# ANCIENT WORLD IN MINUTES

CHARLES PHILLIPS

# ANCIENT WORLD IN MINUTES

CHARLES PHILLIPS

Quercus

# CONTENTS

# Introduction

Why do we read about the past? Because it tells us why the world is the way it is today. As American preacher and civil rights leader Martin Luther King Jr declared in November 1954: 'we are made by history'. His words were intended to make his black American congregation take their lives into their hands – not to be passive, constrained by a very difficult past, but to make history. They touch on another key reason to enquire into the past: knowing history helps us avoid repeating past mistakes in taking steps toward a better future.

Our complex modern world has roots going back over many millennia to the 'dawn of history' in the ancient era. Historians plot the events of the distant past through archaeology – physical remains of camps, villages and temples. But their principal source is written evidence. For most, the history of the ancient world begins with the development of farming, the establishment of towns and cities and the invention of writing.

Beginning at roughly the same time, a few millennia BCE, ancient history runs to a different end point in different cultures. In Europe, for example, historians view the deposition of the last Roman emperor in the West, Romulus Augustulus, in 476 CE as the end of the ancient world. This ushered in transformative changes in the West. But in the Americas, there was cultural continuity from the 1st millennium BCE onward. It makes sense here to view the ancient world as continuing to the Spanish invasion in the 16th century.

This book provides 200 vivid snapshots of the ancient world in which so many modern ideas and inventions have their origins. Our coverage takes in key mathematical breakthroughs in ancient India, and the invention of paper and tea-drinking in China. We touch on mystery: the ziggurats of Mesopotamia, Egyptian pyramids and Nazca Lines in Peru. You'll also find all the glory of Ancient Greece and Rome – including Homer and Sappho, the first Olympic Games, the love affair of Mark Antony and Cleopatra and the building of the Colosseum. My hope is that these snapshots of our shared past will inspire you to read further in the knowledge that history illuminates the way forward in the future.

Charles Phillips

# What is civilization?

**S**ix great civilizations emerged independently from 10,000 BCE onward, as the Neolithic Revolution – the transition from hunting and gathering to a settled existence based on farming – took effect around the world. They were in Mesopotamia, Egypt, the Indus Valley, China, the Andes and Mesoamerica. Historians debate what civilization means, but most agree it is associated with the establishment of towns and cities and trade between them, the emergence of a social elite engaged in administration and religious activities, and the use of writing.

The movement to farming allowed food surpluses, which freed people to engage in cultural life and administer trade. Some argue that people were not civilized until they accepted a central authority (state) that controlled or monopolized the use of force, and until they developed skills in metalworking. Another key element is the emergence of mathematics, initially through devising calendars to keep track of seasons and plot planting cycles, and geometry for building temples, altars and palaces.

Giant statues of Pharaoh Amenhotep III on the plain near modern Luxor, Egypt, stand as a 3,400-year-old testament to the organizing power of civilizations.

# Agriculture

Over a period of 5,000 years, beginning around 10,000 BCE, many peoples around the world turned from hunter-gatherer lifestyles to an existence based on herding animals and growing crops. The process began in the so-called Fertile Crescent — extending from the Nile delta through modern Jordan, Syria, parts of southern Turkey and Iraq — where people started raising goats, pigs and sheep and cultivating wheat. Around 8000 BCE people were cultivating rice in the Yangtze River valley in southern China and the Ganges River valley in India. By 6000 BCE farming had spread to Europe, appearing first at Knossos on Crete, in Thessaly, mainland Greece and, shortly afterward, in the Balkans. In the Americas, people domesticated maize in Central America and grew potatoes in the central Andes around 5000 BCE. Initially, farmers worked the land with hand ploughs but, by about 6000 BCE, they began to use domesticated oxen to pull a scratch plough, which greatly increased the crop yields. The oldest known ploughed field is at Kalibangan, Indus Valley, dating back to around 3000 BCE.

# Religion

Food surpluses produced by agriculture freed people to spend time away from seeking sustenance. Individuals were also free to specialize, and one key specialist was the priest. People who experienced natural disasters – crops ruined by flood or fire, earthquakes, tsunamis or total eclipses – or the sudden death of loved ones probably reached the conclusion that unseen powers were at work. Priests were those who performed sacrifices and other rituals to win the blessing of these gods, ancestors or nature spirits.

In many early cultures, people came to believe that rituals had to be performed perfectly to avert disaster and ensure the continuance of everyday events like the Sun rising. The Vedic priests of India, for example, memorized the words of sacred hymns, and were experts in building altars and performing animal sacrifices. Others continued to follow shamanism. Shamans were healers and spiritual adepts who claimed to communicate with spirits and accompany the dead to the afterlife.

The monoliths at Göbekli Tepe, Turkey, the world's oldest known surviving temple, are estimated as dating to the 9th–10th millennium BCE.

# Towns, cities
# and government

Early farmers lived in clusters of houses near the fields they worked. These villages included granaries for storing excess crops for use later in the year and burial grounds for the dead. The first towns followed soon after the adoption of farming and the growth of religious rituals. By 8000 BCE, Jericho in the West Bank was established as a town, enclosed by a wall and home to perhaps 2,000–3,000 people. The settlement's walls suggest the need for defence against raiding groups.

Cities had an element of planned, rather than random, growth. The first cities, Uruk and Eridu, emerged c.5000 BCE in the Sumerian civilization of Mesopotamia. Growing rich on agriculture, they became centres of far-reaching trade, and developed forms of government to manage their trading and irrigation networks. Society was increasingly hierarchical: the king ruled as a god and lived in isolation among his family, served by officials and priests. As the symbolic head of state, the ruler commanded troops when cities came into conflict with rivals.

Babylon grew from being a small Akkadian city *c.*2300 BCE, to become the largest city in the world from *c.*1770–1670 BCE.

# Bronze

For thousands of years people had fashioned tools from animal bone, wood and stone, in what historians call the Stone Age. The transition to metal tools and weapons was a major breakthrough that brought about many changes, both positive and negative, including trade and increased conflict.

Metalworking began as early as 6500 BCE: artisans in Anatolia (Turkey) began working pure copper to make ornaments that have been found in rich graves. Soon, vibrant commercial networks were thriving and the trade in copper contributed to the rise of Mesopotamian towns and cities. By c.3500 BCE, the making of cast copper weapons and tools was well established. Later, people began to work bronze, an alloy of copper and tin that is much harder than copper and could be used to make more practical weapons, armour and tools. Bronze-working began in the Middle East and China before 3000 BCE and spread slowly, reaching Britain and northern Europe by c.1900 BCE.

A bronze axe from the Shang Dynasty (1600–1046 BCE), China. Ownership of such an object would confer power and military authority.

# Writing

Six ancient civilizations independently developed the ability to represent spoken language using written symbols, beginning in Mesopotamia. By the late 4th millennium BCE, accountants in Sumer were cutting pictorial images into clay tablets as a way of keeping tallies. Over time, they developed more abstract symbols that represented units of spoken Sumerian. Historians call this first written language 'cuneiform' from the Latin meaning 'wedge-shaped' (opposite).

Not long afterwards, c.3000 BCE, the Ancient Egyptians developed hieroglyphs – picture characters that represent both objects and sounds, or groups of sounds. Different writing systems were developed in India, c.3000–2600 BCE, on soapstone seals and in China on oracle bones by c.1200 BCE. Mesoamerican Zapotec (c.600 BCE) and Maya (c.400 BCE) cultures also invented their own writing. In a sense the development of writing marks the beginning of history, because it makes it possible to create a lasting record of rulers, conquests and other events.

# Trade and administration

**F**ood surpluses and craft activities, such as copper- and bronzeworking, in the 3rd millennium BCE, boosted trade networks. Emerging cities in the agriculturally rich lands of Mesopotamia traded grain for raw materials, such as pure copper, copper ores and tin, that their craftsmen needed for metalworking. They also imported precious stones and building materials. In this era, markets were established in towns and cities, and a new class of administrators and merchants oversaw the burgeoning trade network.

The great cultures of Mesopotamia and the Indus Valley were trading with one another by c.3000 BCE. The Indus Valley cities also traded gems and beads by sea through their port of Lothal, with Egypt. In Shang-Dynasty China, merchants traded shells and jade over long distances on the Yellow and Yangtze rivers, but generally not further than Korea and Japan. Later, the first settlers in the Cyclades and the Phoenicians of Lebanon greatly prospered through sea trade.

This cuneiform tablet from *c.*2040 BCE is a receipt for the sale of goats.

# Calendars

Ancient peoples devised calendars to track the movements of the Sun and Moon, the return of the seasons and the agricultural cycle. The oldest-known calendar dates to c.2700 BCE, when the people of Sumer were using a lunar count, based on 12 months of 29 or 30 days, that began on the first sighting of the New Moon. To align their lunar year of around 354 days with the solar year of around 365 days they added an extra month periodically. The months were usually named after the festivals that took place during them, and the year began before or after harvest. From c.2400 BCE, they also used the royal year to record events in a king's reign. This began when a new king offered the first harvest gathering to the gods. The Egyptians followed a lunar calendar, but also a solar civil calendar with 12 months of 30 days – with five days outside the schedule at the end of every year. The Maya combined a 365-day cycle (eighteen 20-day months, plus five unnamed days) with a 260-day ritual calendar, and the two together comprised a 'Calendar Round' of 18,980 days.

# Iron

Beginning about 1200 BCE in the Near East, southeast Europe and India, metalworkers began to make tools, weapons and coins from iron rather than bronze. One theory is that a disruption of trade routes in 1300–1200 BCE led to a shortage of tin, so Near-East artisans had to look beyond bronze. Around the same time they developed smelting and smithing abilities to make iron and steel implements. At one time historians held that the Hittites had a monopoly on making iron weapons, which were taken and disseminated by the Sea Peoples who swept away Hittite power, but this theory is largely discredited.

The transition to iron took place at different times in different areas – c.1200 BCE in India, c.800–600 BCE in central and northern Europe, c.600 BCE in China, and not until c.300 BCE in Korea and Japan. In traditional accounts, the Iron Age was an era of great movements of migrants armed with iron weapons – such as the Dorians, who invaded Greece and eliminated the Mycenaean and Minoan civilizations, ushering in the Greek Dark Ages.

The development of iron technology permitted large-scale production of objects through casting or striking, such as this Celtic coin.

# Mathematics

People probably started counting to work out calendars. A baboon bone dated as early as 35,000 BCE and found in the Lebombo Mountains, southern Africa, is marked with 29 notches, thought to represent the nights of the Moon's cycle. When settlers began to herd animals and store crops, or build palaces and public buildings, they developed mathematics to keep tally and understand the geometry of building. Written evidence in cuniform, dating from c.3000 BCE, shows that these were the main uses of mathematics at the time.

In c.1800 BCE, a clay tablet (opposite) was carved with Pythagorean triples – trios of perfect solutions to the Pythagorean theorem of right-angled triangles. These show that Mesopotamians had this knowledge long before Pythagoras. Earlier, people in Peru used complex mathematical ideas in quipus (knotted-string memory devices that recorded people and possessions) and calendar information. Archaeologists have found a quipu at the Norte Chico culture site of Caral dated to 3000 BCE.

# Uruk and Sumeria

One of the world's first cities, Uruk, was a major centre of the Sumerian civilization of southern Mesopotamia, in modern Iraq, southwestern Turkey and eastern Syria. On this site stood a city with brick walls 10 km (6 miles) long and a ziggurat, or stepped tower, supporting a temple to the sky god Anu. The sky goddess Inanna was also worshipped in the city, which according to myth was built by and home to the legendary king Gilgamesh.

Sumer developed a stratified society, with urban centres like Uruk, bureaucrats and full-time soldiers replacing a life based on small farming villages. Sumerian Uruk blossomed, particularly in c.3500–2900 BCE, when copper, silver and gold were worked there, and craftsmen made beautiful amulets and seals. At this time Uruk was one of around 12 city-states in Sumer – others included Nippur, Lagash and Kish. The city endured through to the Parthian era (247 BCE–224 CE) and many foreign kings, including Cyrus the Great and Darius I of the Achaemenid Empire, left their mark on it.

Sumerian ruins at Al–Zibliya
in modern Iraq

# Epic of Gilgamesh

A legendary king, Gilgamesh is the hero of the ancient world's oldest surviving work of literature. The Epic of Gilgamesh describes how this part-divine, part-human warrior fought, defeated and befriended a wild man named Enkidu, sent by the gods to humble him. He rejected the advances of the love goddess Ishtar, then defeated the divine bull she despatched to kill him. As punishment, the gods brought about the death of Enkidu, and Gilgamesh, plunged into grief, failed in his attempt to discover the secret of eternal life. But he achieved immortality of a sort through his undying fame.

The oldest fragments of the epic date to the 18th century BCE. Its most complete version, from the 13th–10th centuries BCE, was found in the library of the Assyrian king Ashurbanipal, who reigned 668–627 BCE (opposite). The epic also contains a flood myth, in which the world is destroyed in a great deluge. This is mirrored in the biblical story of Noah and the religious traditions of the Ancient Maya, Hinduism, and Norse and Aboriginal mythologies.

# Susa

Susa was capital of the ancient kingdom of Elam, in modern southwestern Iran. Classical writers called the kingdom Susiana, from the name of the capital city. Elam had three periods of prominence in the ancient world: Old (from *c.*2700 BCE), Middle (from *c.*1285 BCE) and Late (from 742 BCE), and finally became a *satrapy* (province) of the Persian Achaemenid Empire, with Susa being the capital of Darius I from 522 BCE.

In the Old period, Elam was overrun by Shulgi, king of Ur in the 21st century BCE, and again by Hammurabi of Babylon in the 18th century BCE, but both times had revenge. In the Middle period, Elam was a great military power, capturing Babylon and carrying home an inscribed column bearing the law code of Hammurabi (see page 44). In this period, *c.*1250 BCE, King Untash-Gal built a great palace and ziggurat with a base 105 m (344 ft) square at Dur Untashi, near Susa. In the Late Period, the Elamites tried to intervene in Mesopotamia with little success; Ashurbanipal looted and destroyed Susa in 647 BCE.

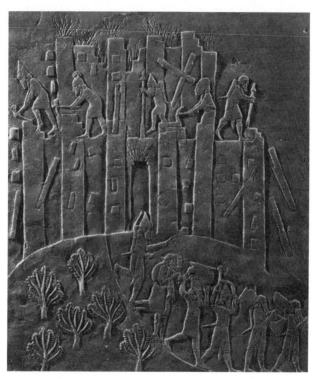

A relief from Ashurbanipal's palace at Nineveh depicts the destruction of Susa.

# Sargon and the Akkadian Empire

Sargon of Akkad is known as the world's first empire builder. Ruling in the 24th century BCE, he conquered the whole of southern Mesopotamia, together with areas of Syria, western Iran and Anatolia to form the Akkadian Empire. The many peoples of Mesopotamia looked back to him as father of their military traditions. From his capital at Agade, which has never been identified, merchants traded as far as the Indus Valley, Crete and perhaps mainland Greece.

Little is known of Sargon's life. Legend has it that as a baby he was found floating in a basket and raised by a humble gardener, before becoming cup-bearer to the king of Kish, in northern Sumer. He won a great military victory over Lugalzagesi of Uruk and took control of this king's many client rulers in Mesopotamia, then embarked on further conquests. He dedicated his capital and his success to the goddess Ishtar, Akkadian counterpart of the Sumerian goddess Inanna, also known as Astarte.

Sargon II (right) and dignitary, from the palace at Dur-Sharrukin in Assyria (now Khorsabad, Iraq).

# Lagash

To the east of Uruk, at the meeting of the Tigris and Euphrates rivers, Lagash was an important city under rulers named Ur-baba and Gudea in c.2100 BCE. Gudea (opposite) laid irrigation channels and built temples in many places, including Uruk and Ur. He called himself 'god of Lagash' and no fewer than 26 statues of him have been found in excavations at the nearby site of Girsu (modern Telloh). His kingdom maintained far-reaching trade, importing cedar wood and quarried stone from Lebanon, copper from Arabia and gold from Sinai.

Other relics from his reign include a pair of terracotta cylinders, respectively 61 cm (24 in) and 56 cm (22 in) tall. Their cuneiform inscriptions in the Sumerian language narrate a myth about the building of a temple to Ningirsu. This city god was associated with spring rains and linked particularly to Lagash. Historians have also identified the god as an aspect of the Mesopotamian god of law and agriculture, Ninurta. After Gudea's reign, Lagash declined in importance and influence.

# Ur and the ziggurat builders

The city of Ur (modern Tell el-Muqayyar, in Iraq) was the capital of an empire already under its third dynasty of kings, when Ur-Nammu (reigned 2112–2095 BCE) built its celebrated ziggurat. The vast stepped pyramid bore a shrine to the city's patron and divine ruler, the Moon god Nanna. It measured 64x46 m (210x150 ft) and probably stood 30 m (98 ft) high. Many ziggurats were built in the ancient cities of Assyria, Babylonia and Sumer, over more than 1,500 years from around 2200–500 BCE. Around 25 survive today.

Constructed of mud brick and faced with baked brick, they had no internal chambers. Some apparently did not provide a way to ascend to the top, but in others there was either a triple stairway on one face – as at Ur – or a spiral ramp. The ziggurat supporting the temple of the god Marduk in Babylon has been linked by some to the biblical Tower of Babel. After a long period of relative neglect, the Babylonian king Nebuchadrezzar II rebuilt the city of Ur in the 6th century BCE.

An aerial photograph shows the surviving ruins of Ur.

# Shamshi-Adad,
# King of Assyria

**S**hamshi-Adad I seized power in *c.*1809 BCE in the kingdom of Assyria and built an empire covering most of Syria and Anatolia, and all of Upper Mesopotamia. This was a precursor of later Assyrian empires (see page 48). Historians believe Shamshi-Adad was a member of the Semitic Amorite people from Syria. He moved the Assyrian capital from the ancient city of Ashur to Shubat-Enlil, in the north of modern Syria. At Shubat-Enlil, meaning the 'house of the god Enlil' in Akkadian, he built a palace, temple and a gated city wall.

A vigorous military campaigner, Shamshi-Adad occupied and placed his sons on the thrones of Mari in Syria, which was on an important caravan route, and Ekallatum, a still-unidentified site on the Tigris. The conquerer declared himself 'King of All', the title used by Sargon of Akkad, and inscriptions claim that he raised stelae (inscribed columns) on the Mediterranean coast. In Nineveh, Shamshi-Adad rebuilt the Ishtar temple, and he also constructed a great palace in Ashur.

Ancient Akkadian seal depicting the goddess
Ishtar and her supreme courier, Ninshubur.

# Abraham

The biblical figure Abraham was a Hebrew patriarch and a major figure in Judaism, Christianity and Islam. He has been tentatively identified by historians as leader of a tribal migration from the Mesopotamian city of Ur to the region of Hebron (today on the West Bank, south of Jerusalem) sometime between 2000 BCE and 1500 BCE. In the biblical account he follows the call of God (Yahweh) to leave home and found a new nation in the land of Canaan, between Egypt and Syria. Aged 100, his wife Sarah miraculously gives birth to a son, Isaac, heir to God's promise. Abraham finally died aged 175, and is buried in the cave of Machpelah, near Hebron.

Historians have traced the migration up through modern Iraq, crossing the Euphrates into Turkey, then through Syria and across the Jordan River to Jerusalem and Hebron. The migrants lived as shepherds, as they took a route now thought to have followed major religious centres for the Moon god Nanna, or Sin, and the Canaanite deity Baal-Berith ('Lord of the Covenant').

# Hammurabi the Great

Hammurabi the Great – the sixth king of a Semitic Akkadian dynasty – extended Babylon's power across Mesopotamia in the early 18th century BCE and created one of the world's oldest-known law codes. In forming the first Babylonian Empire, he repelled an invasion by Elam, took control of the kingdom of Larsa (southern Mesopotamia), crushed Eshnunna (central Mesopotamia), then defeated Mari and Assyrian ruler Ishme-Dagan I to win control of the northern part of the region.

His law code, dated to c.1742 BCE, was written on inscribed stone slabs or stelae for public display (opposite). It prescribed severe punishments: for stealing, death; for fraud, paying ten times the amount defrauded; for slander, marking the brow. The inscription states that Hammurabi was selected by the gods to receive the law, just as God chose Moses in Jewish tradition. There are enough likenesses between the code of Hammurabi and Jewish laws for historians to suggest both are derived from an older code in a shared Semitic tradition.

Hammurabi receives his laws from the enthroned sun god Shamash.

# Hittites

From their capital Hattusa (modern Bogazkoy, central Turkey) the Hittites under Hattusilis I, and his grandson Mursilis I, took control of Anatolia and northern Syria, and raided Babylon in the 17th century BCE. They created what historians call the Hittite Old Kingdom. Mursilis also conducted a campaign against the Hurrians on the upper Euphrates, and carried back great riches and many prisoners to Hattusa. The Old Kingdom ruler Hantilis fortified the capital, and sections of the ancient city wall can still be seen today. Around 300 years later, their successors – notably Suppiluliumas I from c.1380 BCE – created the empire of the Hittite New Kingdom. They remained an important international power until the 12th century BCE. The Hittite king Muwatalli fought Egyptian pharaoh Ramses II in the celebrated Battle of Kadesh in 1299 BCE and then, in c.1286 BCE, Hattusili III signed a diplomatic treaty with Ramses incorporating a dynastic marriage in which a Hittite princess married the pharaoh. The empire collapsed in the face of invasions by the Sea Peoples, c.1200 BCE, and eventually became part of Assyria.

Seal of the Hittite ruler Tarkummuwa. This famous bilingual inscription (c.1400 BCE) provided the first clues for deciphering Hittite hieroglyphs.

# Kassites

The Kassites ruled Babylon for more than 400 years from *c.*1570 BCE. We know little of their rise to power except that they probably came from the Zagros Mountains in Iran, established themselves in northern Babylonia in the 18th century BCE and came to power in Babylon following its defeat by the Hittites. Close to Babylon, the Kassites founded their capital city, Dur-Kurigalzu (now Aqarquf in Iraq) – named for the king Kurigalzu – and built a great ziggurat, three temples and a palace with fine wall paintings.

They held the horse to be sacred and pioneered the use of moulded bricks to create relief decoration on buildings. They are also known for the custom of erecting so-called boundary stones (opposite) that recorded the gifting of territory by the king to those whose service he valued. These were carved with images of deities who were believed to safeguard the contract. In the 12th century BCE, the Kassites were driven from Babylon by a resurgent Elam and returned to the Zagros.

# Egypt unified

**N**armer was the first pharaoh of a united Egypt, *c.*3000 BCE. Some modern historians argue that he was a legend and actually represents a series of rulers who together unified Egypt, laying the foundations for a kingdom that gave rise to one of the ancient world's greatest civilizations. The 3rd century BCE Egyptian historian Manetho called him Menes; modern historians identify him as Narmer or Aha – kings whose tombs were excavated at Abydos in Upper Egypt. In traditional accounts, Narmer combined Lower Egypt (roughly the fertile Nile delta) and Upper Egypt (roughly the Nile river valley).

A king list, called the Turin Papyrus and compiled under Pharaoh Ramses II (reigned 1279–1213 BCE), said this king, whom it calls 'Meni', diverted the River Nile and founded the Ancient Egyptian capital of Memphis. The 'Narmer Palette' (a ceremonial siltstone, opposite) shows the king triumphing over enemies and wearing the white and red crowns of Upper and Lower Egypt – signifying that he stamped his authority on a unified kingdom.

# Hieroglyphs

Ancient Egyptian hieroglyphs date back to 3000 BCE. Ivory tablets and clay jars with picture writing on them were placed in tombs at this time, probably to identify the deceased. Their name derives from the Greek for 'sacred carvings', so-called because of their frequent appearance in temples and tombs; the Egyptians called them *medou netjer* ('words of the gods') and believed they had been invented by the god of writing, Thoth. There were three main types: phonograms (representation of sounds), logograms (representations of words) and determinatives (clarifications of meaning). One set of 24 phonograms represented single consonants, while another, numbering several hundred, represented two or three consonant sounds combined. The names of kings on monuments, or lists of rulers in royal dynasties, were written within an oval enclosure, called a cartouche, that was supposed to function as a protection – for the Egyptians believed written words held great power. Saying aloud a name written in hieroglyphs in a tomb inscription made the person live again.

# Zoser and the
# Old Kingdom

Pharaoh Zoser, who ruled c.2650–c.2575 BCE, was the
second king of the 3rd Dynasty of the Old Kingdom – the
first flowering of the Ancient Egyptian civilization. This was
a time of great prosperity following the unification of Egypt.
Records show that Zoser sent expeditions to the Sinai
Peninsula and subdued locals there. He was the first pharaoh
to live only at Memphis, playing a part in the city becoming
the capital of the Old Kingdom rulers.

Zoser also built the first great pyramid of Ancient Egypt
(opposite). Previously, tombs and funerary buildings had been
rectangular with flat roofs, made of mud-brick and stone.
Zoser and his vizier built a six-stepped pyramid surrounded by
a complex of limestone shrines, at Saqqarah, outside Memphis,
in which he was eventually buried. The Old Kingdom continued
for around 500 years until c.2130 BCE, probably due to weak
rulers, environmental catastrophes and famine, power passed
to pharaohs based at Heracleopolis in Upper Egypt.

# Pyramids and mummification

Later pharaohs of the Old Kingdom followed in the steps of Zoser in building pyramids as funerary monuments and royal tombs. The three most celebrated are at Giza on the outskirts of modern Cairo (opposite) and were erected from the 26th century BCE onward. The largest and oldest, the Great Pyramid, was built by Pharaoh Khufu of the 4th Dynasty (c. 2575–c. 2465 BCE). Its square base measures 230 m (755 ft) on each side, and originally it rose to a height of 147 m (482 ft). The other two were built by Khufu's son, Khafre, and by Khafre's successor, Menkaure. Pyramids contained the pharaoh's tomb and were set within architectural groupings, including a mortuary temple and a pavilion or valley temple – often connected by canal to the Nile. They were surrounded by smaller pyramids for the burial of lesser royals. Buried bodies were mummified. This embalming process consisted chiefly of taking out the inner organs, using resin to treat the body and then wrapping it in linen bandages. The mummies were buried with the wealth and supplies the pharaoh was thought to need in the afterlife.

# Ptah-hotep's *Maxims*

Ptah-hotep, a vizier in the reign of Pharaoh Djedkare Isesi, wrote the world's oldest surviving book of philosophy in the 25th century BCE. He laid out his *Maxims* primarily to instruct young men destined for government service in correct behaviour, emphasizing that the highest virtue was to obey one's father or superior in rank.

He also stressed the importance of listening, and urged the young men to develop an ability to be silent, if necessary, to be faithful in doing their duty and to be humble. He said a person's conduct should be straightforward and warned against gossiping, because people respect those who hold their own counsel. The book is an example of 'wisdom literature', like *The Instructions of Kagemni* (opposite), from the reign of Pharaoh Sneferu (reigned 2613–2589 BCE) and the biblical book of *Proverbs*. The *Maxims* survive in four copies, only one of which is complete. It was discovered in Thebes in 1847 by French archaeologist Émile Prisse d'Avennes.

# Mentuhotep II and the Middle Kingdom

**M**entuhotep II (opposite) reunited Egypt after a prolonged period of weakness when there were rival rulers in Thebes and Heracleopolis, the main cities of Upper and Lower Egypt. After 60 years of war between the two cities, Mentuhotep defeated Heracleopolis in the 14th year of his reign (around 1994 BCE). This brought to an end the era historians call the First Intermediate Period, which had followed the Old Kingdom (c.2575–c.2130 BCE), and ushered in the Middle Kingdom (c.1938–c.1630 BCE). Mentuhotep II made Thebes the capital and restored Egypt to prosperity. After he reunited the country, his subjects viewed him as a god. He centralized power, creating governors of Lower and Upper Egypt to control regional rulers who had become independent-minded. Mentuhotep's military campaigns also took the kingdom into Canaan and Nubia. He was a great builder of temples and erected a superb complex around his tomb at Thebes. Decorated by local Theban artists, it contains some of the earliest images of the god Amun Ra, deity of the Middle Kingdom rulers.

# Amenemhat III

Under Amenemhat III (1818-1770 BCE), Middle Kingdom Egypt was at its peak. The pharaoh's engineers built an artificial lake to control the flooding of the Nile. Lake Moeris, which occupied the al-Fayyum depression near Cairo, contained 13 billion m³ (460 billion cubic feet) of water and reclaimed more than 62,000 hectares (153,000 acres) of agricultural land from the river. A canal linked the lake with the river.

He celebrated this achievement by building a labyrinth – hailed by Greek geographer Strabo as a wonder of the ancient world. The labyrinth probably functioned as an all-in-one palace, administrative centre and mortuary temple. He also raised two colossi of himself, noted by Greek historian Herodotus. Amenemhat's reign was largely peaceful and trade flourished. He drew great wealth from turquoise mines in Sinai and amethyst mines at Wadi el-Hudi. Goods associated with him have been found as far north as the seaport of Byblos, Lebanon. He was finally interred in a pyramid at Hawara.

# Hyksos rule

A line of kings originally from Palestine ruled Egypt in *c.*1630–1523 BCE. They were called 'Hyksos' by 3rd century BCE Egyptian historian Manetho, which probably means 'rulers from foreign lands'. The arrival of the Hyksos marked what historians call the Second Intermediate Period between the Middle Kingdom (*c.*1938–*c.*1630 BCE) and the New Kingdom (*c.*1539–1075 BCE).

Their rise followed the immigration into Egypt of Palestinians who were adept with the compound bow and metal weapons and skilled at using horses and chariots. They worshipped the Egyptian storm and desert god Seth, and settled mainly in Avaris in the eastern Nile delta, from where they rose to prominence when the pharaohs of the 13th and 14th Egyptian dynasties lost their grip on power. The Hyksos ruled for just over a century until they were ousted by Pharaoh Ahmose I (opposite), founder of the 18th Dynasty. Ahmose captured Egypt's traditional capital Memphis before leading a waterborne attack on Avaris and driving the Hyksos back to Palestine.

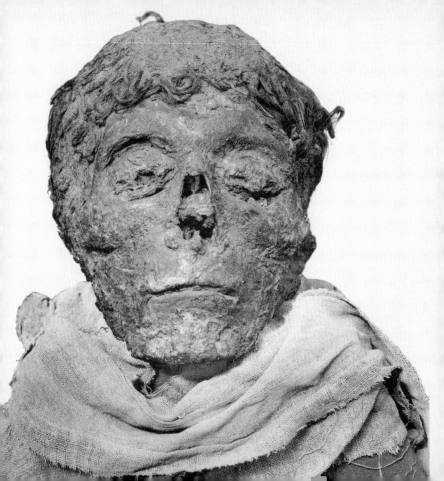

# Valley of the Kings and the New Kingdom

Founded by Thutmose I, the 18th Dynasty marked the beginning of the New Kingdom (*c.*1539–1075 BCE), the period following the rule of the Hyksos in the Second Intermediate Period. The New Kingdom saw Egypt at its most prosperous and powerful. Pharaohs of the 18th Dynasty began a new tradition in royal burial when they chose to be laid to rest in a barren valley west of the River Nile at Thebes, in what came to be known as the Valley of the Kings. Seeking to prevent their tombs being plundered by robbers, they built burial chambers accessed by a descending corridor leading deep underground. A central chamber contained a stone sarcophagus that enclosed the pharaoh's mummified body, as well as stores of the wealth and supplies the king would need in the afterlife.

The Valley of the Kings contained the tombs of Ramses II, Seti I and Queen Hatshepsut. All were looted in ancient times – except for the tomb of the boy-king Tutankhamun, which was discovered, with its magnificent grave goods intact, in 1922.

Nefertiti (c.1370–c.1330 BCE), Great Royal Wife of Akhenaten, is well known from her iconic portrait bust, a rare survival recovered by archaeologists from a sculptor's workshop.

# Queen Hatshepsut

Hatshepsut, daughter of Thutmose I, ruled Egypt as pharaoh in the 15th century BCE, with all the titles and power of a male ruler. Her statues and portraits showed her with a man's body, and wearing the pharaoh's regalia – kilt, crown and false beard. She achieved unprecedented power for a woman in this era. Hatshepsut was married to her half-brother, Pharaoh Thutmose II. After his death Hatshepsut took power, first as regent for Thutmose III – her half-brother's son with a queen from his harem – and finally in her own right in 1473–1458 BCE. She ruled through personally selected officials in key government positions, notably Senenmut, who may have been her lover. Images at the funerary temple she built at Dayr al-Bahri, Thebes, suggest Hatshepsut oversaw a military campaign in Nubia and a trading expedition by sea to Punt (modern Somalia/Djibouti) that brought back ebony, gold and myrrh trees. She was buried in the Valley of the Kings in her father's tomb, which she specially extended. When Thutmose III came to power after her death, Hatshepsut's name was removed from the king list and her monuments were defaced.

# Akhenaten

Pharaoh Amenhotep IV (reigned 1353–1336 BCE) established a new cult of the Sun's disc Aton in Egypt that some historians say is the world's first example of monotheism. He rejected the established worship of Amun and demanded the god's image be removed from temples. Instead, temple carvings show Amenhotep and his beautiful queen Nefertiti being showered with blessings by Aton. As part of this new but short-lived religion, he changed his name to Akhenaten ('Of Benefit to Aton') and built a new capital called Akhetaten – now known as Tell el-Amarna – beside the Nile river, around 300 km (186 miles) north of Thebes. It is centred on a huge temple to Aton. Akhenaten oversaw a new style in the arts, now called the Amarna style. The pharaoh and his circle were shown with projecting jaw, swollen belly, large thighs and hips and very thin legs. These features are particularly noticeable in colossi representing the pharaoh at Karnak, and some show him without male sex organs. The new religion did not survive Akhenaten's death.

# Tutankhamun

Tutankhamun is probably the most famous of all Egyptian pharaohs – on account of his tomb, discovered in 1922 in the Valley of the Kings. In a small burial room, his mummified body was found within three coffins, the outer two of hammered gold on wooden frames and the inner one of solid gold. The young pharaoh wore a golden portrait mask, also with amulets and jewellery. He was the successor of Akhenaten.

His short reign (1333–1323 BCE) began when he was a boy. Relying on Ay, an official, and Horemheb, a general, as advisers, Tutankhamun rolled back the religious revolution of Akhenaten, restoring the temples and images of the old gods. He moved his seat of rule from Akhenaten's capital at Akhetaton to Memphis and built a palace at Karnak, a temple in Thebes and the Colonnade to the Temple at Luxor. Tutankhamun may have been Akhenaten's son, and he certainly married Akhenaten's daughter, the princess Ankhesenpaaten. Dying unexpectedly and without a designated heir, he was succeeded by Ay.

# Ramses II

In a 66-year reign between 1279 BCE and 1213 BCE, Ramses II led a series of military campaigns, built temples and raised a succession of colossal statues of himself. As a young prince, Ramses accompanied his father, Seti I, on his campaigns on Egypt's northern frontiers and, once pharaoh, he continued these wars, notably against the Hittites and Libyans.

Ramses built a new capital Per Ramessu, in the northeastern delta, celebrated for its orchards and gardens, and laid out in four quarters under the protection of Amun, Seth, Wadjet and the Syrian goddess Astarte. Two famous temples built during his reign were cut from the cliff at Abu Simbel in Nubia (southern Egypt). He finished the Hypostyle Hall at Karnak begun by his father, which has vast carvings of Seti and Ramses in their war chariots. The third king of the 19th Dynasty (1292–1190 BCE), Ramses was the embodiment of regal power. No fewer than nine kings of the 20th Dynasty (1190–1075 BCE) took his name, and Ancient Egyptian historians called him 'the Great'.

# Book of the Dead

Ancient Egyptians believed that after their death they would need magical formulae and spells to pass through the underworld and thrive in the afterlife. These were written on papyrus rolls and placed in tombs, and are collectively known to historians as the Book of the Dead. Some described gods, while others were intended to help the deceased control their new surroundings. One sets out the Weighing of the Heart ritual, in which the dead person's heart was weighed against the feather of the goddess Ma'at (representing what was true).

The Egyptian name for the Book of the Dead is translated as the 'Book of Coming Forth by Day'. Derived from older traditions – the Pyramid Texts of c.2400 BCE, where the formulae were written on the walls of chambers within pyramids, and the Coffin Texts of c.2100 BCE, where the spells were written on royal coffins – the papyrus copies of the Book of the Dead were written by scribes from c.1550 BCE until as late as c.50 BCE.

# Exodus

The most likely historical setting for the events of the biblical book of Exodus is the reign of Pharaoh Ramses II. The book describes how the Israelites were delivered from slavery in Egypt by the power of God and the leadership of Moses (opposite). The Israelites may have been forced labour in the building of Ramses' great new city of Per Ramessu (see page 74).

The biblical account tells that Moses – an Israelite born in Egypt and raised at the pharaoh's court – relayed to the pharaoh God's words, 'Let my people go!' The pharaoh only made them work harder. God visited ten plagues upon the Egyptians, and Moses led the Israelites to liberty when God parted the waters of the Red Sea, sending them crashing down on the pursuing Egyptian chariots and cavalry. After long wanderings, the Israelites settled in Canaan (modern Palestine). Some scholars think the words Yam Suph, translated as 'Red Sea', should be given as the 'Sea of Reeds' and referred to a lake, now dried up, north of the Gulf of Suez.

# Ramses III

Ramses III won three great victories over armies attempting to invade Ancient Egypt. The most famous, in c.1175 BCE, was over the Sea Peoples. This fearsome band of warlike migrants – possibly from the Mediterranean islands and Anatolia – had swept all before them. Ramses defeated them on land in a battle in what is now southern Palestine, then overcame the invaders' navy after ambushing their ships in the Nile Delta.

The two other invasions that Ramses resisted both came from Libya. The Battle of the Delta is celebrated in relief carvings in his mortuary temple at Medinet Habu in Thebes. He also made additions to the Theban temple at Karnak, and imported copper from Sinai and gold from Nubia. Like Hatshepsut, he despatched a seaborne trading expedition to Punt. Ramses III's reign of 30-odd years was brought to a violent end when his throat was cut in a botched coup d'état in 1156 BCE. He was succeeded by his son Amonhirkopshef, who reigned as Ramses IV.

# Alexandria and Ptolemaic Egypt

Macedonian warrior-general Alexander the Great (356–323 BCE) took control of Egypt in 332 BCE and founded the city of Alexandria on the Mediterranean coast, about 180 km (112 miles) north of Cairo. Following Alexander's death in 323 BCE, Ptolemy, son of a Macedonian nobleman, installed himself as *satrap* or administrator in Egypt, and by 305 BCE was ruling as pharaoh Ptolemy I Soter. He established the Ptolemaic Dynasty that ruled Egypt until Queen Cleopatra committed suicide in 30 BCE. The prosperity of the New Kingdom had been followed by the chaotic Third Intermediate Period (*c.*1075–656 BCE) and Late Period (663–332 BCE), during which the country had been conquered by Assyria in 671 BCE and then Persia in 525 BCE. When Alexander invaded, he found the Egyptians happy to be freed from Persian control, and took power without a battle. One of the major effects of the conquest was the spread of Greek culture, or Hellenization. Alexandria became a centre of Greek learning, and its famous library was created by Ptolemy I. The Pharos (lighthouse) of Alexandria was built in 280–247 BCE.

# Ptolemy V and
# the Rosetta Stone

In 196 BCE, Ptolemy V Epiphanes, ruler of Egypt (205–180 BCE), issued a declaration. It was inscribed on a black granite slab now known as the Rosetta Stone (opposite), which in the 19th century provided the key for deciphering Ancient Egyptian hieroglyphics. Ptolemy V came to the throne aged five, after his dissolute father Ptolemy IV died and his mother was murdered, and was under the control of corrupt courtiers for most of his reign. His decree of 196 BCE detailed his increased donations to temples, covered the release of prisoners and pardon of rebels, and the forgiving of certain debts and taxes. The declaration stone, measuring 114 cm (45 in) high by 72 cm (28 in) across, was engraved using three scripts – Egyptian hieroglyphics, a cursive form of hieroglyphics known as demotic, and Greek. It takes its name from the town of Rosetta (Rashid), northeast of Alexandria, where it was found in August 1799. Englishman Thomas Young and Frenchman Jean-François Champollion led the way in deciphering the stone, making possible the translation of other hieroglyphic texts.

# Norte Chico

The oldest civilization in the Americas was established in coastal north-central Peru, c. 3500–3200 BCE. Its people inhabited cities, including Huaricanga and Caral, with substantial earthwork platform mounds, step pyramids and round sunken plazas. Their culture was peaceful and 'pre-ceramic'. They had very little visual art, but did make and use textiles. Remains indicate that they ate mainly seafood, with beans, sweet potato, squash, guava and a subtropical fruit called lucuma. With no pots for cooking, they probably roasted their food.

Historians think the society was theocratic, with authority derived from the gods. The peoples of different cities shared a pantheon of deities. A c. 2250 BCE gourd appears to show an early image of the Staff God, a hooded, fanged figure usually shown holding a staff in each hand, who was a significant deity for later Andean civilizations, and was worshipped as Viracocha by the Inca. The Norte Chico civilization began to decline c. 1800 BCE, when seemingly people moved away in search of more fertile land.

A standing stone and earthwork mounds at a Caral temple in the dry Supe Valley in Peru.

# Rise of the Maya

The forerunners of the Maya civilization established themselves in the late 3rd millennium BCE on the Pacific coast of Guatemala. These early Maya spread out across Guatemala, to Belize, southeastern Mexico, and the western parts of Honduras and El Salvador. They established villages where they grew staple crops of maize, squashes, chilli peppers and beans.

From c.750 BCE, villages developed into large ceremonial and urban settlements. They built temples covered with stucco masks of their gods, together with monuments and *sacbeob*, or 'white ways' – ceremonial causeways paved with white stone. Nakbe, in the rainforest of Peten, Guatemala, was an early city that contained pyramids and *sacbeob* from the 8th century BCE. At its peak in the 3rd century BCE, nearby El Mirador was home to 250,000 people. Its carefully aligned platforms were topped with pyramids, including the 72-m (236-ft) La Danta temple – one of the ancient world's largest artificial structures.

Stucco mask frieze in Placeres, Mexico, dating from the Mayan Early Classic period (100–600 CE).

# La Florida and Sechin Alto

Great ceremonial centres or temples, such as La Florida and Sechin Alto, were built *c.*1750–1600 BCE in Peru. La Florida, in the Rímac river valley on Peru's central coast, consisted of two terraces each 8–10 m (26–33 ft) high forming a U-shaped platform that enclosed a rectangular plaza and a 17-m (56-ft) tall pyramid, or temple mound, at the centre. It was one of many such temples built in what archaeologists call the Initial Period (1800–800 BCE) in central Peru, which were typically aligned so the plaza's opening faced the headwaters of the river.

Sechin Alto was built on the Sechín river, near the coast of northern Peru. Its pyramidal temple measured 350x300 m (1,150x985 ft) by 35 m (115 ft) tall, and gave onto five plazas, some of which contained sunken circular areas oriented to the northwest. It was part of a vast complex covering up to 400 hectares (990 acres). The stone walls of nearby Cerro Sechin bore around 300 carvings of warrior-priests and the dismembered bodies of their sacrificial victims.

Sechin pendants made of anthracite and mother of pearl.

# Olmec people

The Olmec, who flourished in southern Mexico from c.1200–400 BCE, developed sacred rituals involving bloodletting and human sacrifice, and invented a religious-ceremonial ball game – all features of later civilizations in Mesoamerica. They built a great ceremonial centre at San Lorenzo in the Veracruz rainforest in c.1200 BCE that contained an earthen platform 45 m (148 ft) high, topped with a cone-shaped mound.

San Lorenzo, the centre of the Olmec civilization, later gave way to La Venta on the coast of the Gulf of Mexico, where the Olmec laid out a ceremonial plaza and an enclosure containing tombs, as well as a 30-m (100-ft) clay mound believed to be a representation of a volcano. They carved extraordinary 3-m (10-ft) tall, 28 tonne stone heads (opposite) with flattened faces, thick lips and headgear that looks like a helmet. Combining the features of a jaguar and a baby, they are thought to represent Olmec rulers. Stone carvings found 1,200 km (750 miles) away in El Salvador show the civilization had a wide influence.

# Chavín

Chavín culture spread from a great religious centre established *c.*900 BCE at Chavín de Huantar in the Peruvian Andes. It was influential throughout northern and central Peru for 700 years. The superb temple complex at Chavín de Huantar was built of white granite and black limestone blocks, and decorated with sculptures and carvings. Underground canals drained the highland site, and were shaped so they made a roaring sound like the call of their sacred animal, the jaguar, when filled with rushing water. A maze of tunnels led to a chamber containing the Lanzon, an upright granite sculpture 4.53 m (14 ft 10 in) tall, carved with a snarling mouth.

The Chavín were farmers who ate maize, potatoes and quinoa, as well as llamas. They were skilled in weaving and working gold and their art used birds, jaguars, serpentine and crocodile-like images, and also human figures. Like their forerunners, the Norte Chico culture, they were not warlike – there are no surviving fortifications or artistic representations of warriors.

Wall-mounted carvings of jaguar heads are a common feature of Chavín architecture.

# Poverty Point

The Poverty Point culture flourished across 160 km (100 miles) of the Mississippi River area in North America for around 1,000 years from *c.*1700 BCE. It takes its name from the Poverty Point site in northeastern Louisiana, a city that was home to 4,000–5,000 people. Its people lived as hunter-gatherers, surviving on deer, rabbits, turtles, fish, molluscs, berries, fruits and nuts. They were part of a wide-ranging trade network and items at the site use materials from as far away as the Appalachian Mountains and the Great Lakes.

Six concentric ridges of earth set in a horseshoe shape at Poverty Point, each about 0.9 m (3 ft) tall, were probably the foundations of their dwellings. A nearby T-shaped mound, 20 m (66 ft) high and 210 m (690 ft) wide, appears to represent a bird. Thousands of handmade clay balls have been found at the site, and were probably used to hold heat and aid cooking in the hearths and pits the people used. The Poverty Point site was abandoned *c.*700 BCE, after weather changes led to flooding.

An aerial photograph of the Poverty Point site, Louisiana, USA.

# Paracas culture

The Paracas people who thrived in southern Peru in c.900 BCE–400 CE are known particularly for their burials. They placed the mummified bodies of their elite members in beautiful embroidered cloaks that are some of the finest examples of ancient textile making. In the deep-shaft tombs of the necropolis of Wari Kayan on the Paracas peninsula, they bound the bodies with cord to keep them in a seated position looking out across the bay, and buried them alongside funeral offerings, such as weapons, foods and baskets. Some of the cloaks had images of flying figures, who may have been shamans or perhaps the human spirit after death. The Paracas people lived mostly by fishing, but also grew maize, red peppers, peanuts, yuccas and beans. In addition to being skilled weavers, they made obsidian knives, gold ornaments and fine ceramics, with cream and red colouring. On the north of the Paracas peninsula, a 180-m (590-ft) tall candlestick-shaped geoglyph (ground design), called the Paracas Candelabra, probably represents the lightning stick of the creator god Viracocha.

Detail of embroidery work on a Paracas mummy wrapping

# Zapotec people

The Zapotec people of the Oaxaca Valley of southern Mexico created an empire based on their capital city of Monte Albán, which was established in the 8th century BCE. On a flattened mountaintop, 1 km (0.6 mile) long, they built palaces, temples, imposing stepped stone pyramids and a huge plaza. By 200 BCE, Monte Albán was home to 15,000 people and began to spread to terraced land on adjoining hills. The height of its influence came in 200 BCE–200 CE, when there were 15 separate residential areas.

Zapotec peoples made pots with images of the sacred jaguar, practised ritual bloodletting and built a ball court for the religious-cultural ball game typical of Mesoamerica. They traded with the city of Teotihuacan to the northwest and, as early as 600 BCE, were cutting calendrical symbols and hieroglyphs in stone. Their system, in which each glyph represented a syllable, was the first writing in Mesoamerica. Monte Albán endured until around 800 CE, when its power fell away.

Zapotec carving from Monte Albán in southern Mexico.

# Adena culture

The people of the Adena culture of c.500 BCE–100 CE were based in southern Ohio, USA, with associated groups in West Virginia, Indiana and Kentucky. The culture takes its name from the Adena estate near Chillicothe, Ohio, where a major Adena mound was found. Some of the Adena lived in caves but most inhabited villages consisting of round houses with conical willow and bark roofs. They were hunter-gatherers, who made simple pots as well as stone axes and hoes.

There were around 400 Adena sites, with roughly half these in the Ohio Valley. Finds of seashells, mica and copper in camp remains show they traded as far away as the Great Lakes and the Gulf coast. They made large earthworks that historians believe were burial structures and perhaps ceremonial centres. The mounds, up to 90 m (295 ft) across, were built up around bodies and funerary offerings. Objects made from deer antlers and animal jawbones found at these sites were probably used by shamans.

# Great Serpent Mound

The sinuous Great Serpent Mound alongside Ohio Brush Creek in Adams County, Ohio, USA, is the biggest effigy of a serpent in the world. No less than 411 m (1,348 ft) in length, it was built in *c.*320 BCE by people of the Adena culture (see page 102), who were known for building elaborate earthworks. Varying between 30 cm and 100 cm (12–39 in) in height, it follows the contours of the land on which it was built, its seven coils leading to the cha, which is sited near a cliff that rises above a stream. The mouth is open, and reaches around the eastern end of a hollow oval 37 m (121 ft) long – perhaps representing the Sun, or showing the serpent consuming an egg.

Historians have established that the serpent's head and oval are aligned to the sunset at the summer solstice, while some of the coils appear to line up with other key solar and lunar events. Another theory is that it is laid out to mimic the pattern of the constellation Draco. There are Adena graves nearby and it is possible that the mound was designed for use in mortuary rites.

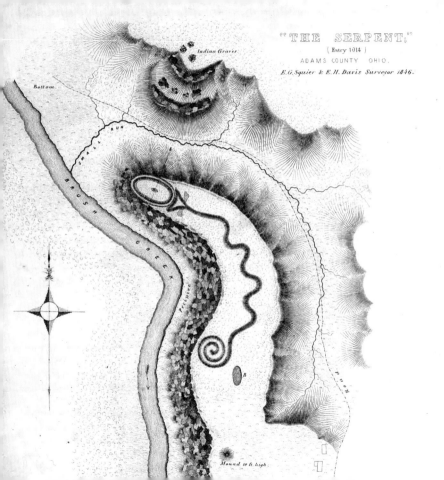

"THE SERPENT,"

(Entry 1014)

ADAMS COUNTY OHIO.

E.G. Squier & E.H. Davis Surveyor 1846.

Indian Graves

Bottom

SMALL RUN

BRUSH CREEK

Precipice

A

B

Mound 10 ft. high

# Nazca Lines

On the windswept Pampa Colorada in southern Peru, the people of the Nazca culture dug vast patterns into the dry surface. Dating from *c.*200 BCE, the images include a spider (opposite), hummingbird, monkey, pelican, killer whale and various trees, plants and abstract spirals. The designs are fully visible only from high above – some are as big as 370 m (1,210 ft) long – and may have been intended to represent constellations and align with their movements for use as an astronomical calendar. Another theory is that they were sacred pathways walked by participants in rituals involving the water and mountain deities worshipped by the Nazca, as many of the designs end in platforms. The Nazca made the lines by removing the red-brown pebbles that cover the plain and creating trenches around 10–15 cm (4–6 in) deep, exposing the lighter, clay earth. The dry climate, with winds that sweep them clean of sand, has preserved them well. The Nazca, who thrived *c.*200 BCE–600 CE, were skilled potters, known for polychrome pots painted white or red, with designs in purple, orange, grey or blue.

# Arawaks in the Caribbean

Arawak migrants from South America travelled along the Orinoco River in Venezuela and made their way to various Caribbean islands *c*.40 CE. Later known as the Taino, they lived on the islands of Cuba, Hispaniola, Jamaica and Puerto Rico in villages of around 3,000 inhabitants. They mainly grew cassava, sweet potatoes, beans and maize, using slash-and-burn cultivation – by clearing trees from wild land and then setting a fire, to create a layer of nutrient-rich ash for growing crops.

They were a peaceful people who revered their chiefs and worshipped a pantheon of ancestor deities and nature spirits. They made belts of dyed cotton, fine pots and carved images in stone, wood, bone and shell. Their ocean-going canoes held more than 100. Some also settled in Trinidad and Tobago, and Grenada. The Taino on Hispaniola were among the first natives encountered by Italian navigator Christopher Columbus in his voyages of discovery to the Americas in 1492 and 1493. Many died from smallpox and other diseases brought from Europe.

Columbus is greeted by Arawak people on his 1492 landing in Hispaniola.

# Moche culture

On the arid northern coast of Peru, the Moche thrived from *c.*100–700 CE. They take their name from their capital city in the Moche river valley, celebrated for its vast Temple of the Sun. This adobe brick stepped pyramid measured 340x136 m (1115x446 ft) by around 41 m (135 ft) tall, and was probably used as a military and administrative centre, and burial site. Nearby is the associated Temple of the Moon, a three-platform structure cut into the hillside that was probably a religious centre. Part of this temple was used in the ritual sacrifice of prisoners of war and the drinking of their blood.

The Moche directed streams pouring down from the Andes into a network of irrigation channels, and grew beans, maize and other crops. They produced exquisite stirrup-spouted water jars decorated with reliefs of animals, humans and gods, and superb gold work. There were dozens of Moche cities across an area extending 400 km (250 miles) along the coast. Climate change may have caused the collapse of their society.

Red-brown earth Moche vessel with bow-shaped handle, from Trujillo, Peru.

# Teotihuacan

The ruins of Teotihuacan, northeast of modern Mexico City, are so impressive that later Aztec pilgrims believed it to be the place where the Sun and Moon were created. The city was built by an unknown people – called Teotihuacanos by historians – and greatly expanded from c.100 BCE onwards by refugees from the eruption of the Cuicuilco volcano in the Valley of Mexico. By 1 CE it had a population of 40,000 and at its height in 500 CE covered more than 20 km² (8 sq miles) and was home to up to 200,000, making it one of the world's largest cities in this era. The 2.4-km (1.5-mile) long, 40-m (130-ft) wide Avenue of the Dead links the most important buildings and points to the sacred Cerro Gordo peak. At its north end is the vast 43-m (140-ft) tall Pyramid of the Moon while to the east of the avenue is the 66-m (217-ft) Pyramid of the Sun. The city's people farmed the surrounding fields, made ceramics and worked with the local green volcanic glass, obsidian, and had far-ranging trade links, including with the Olmec. The priestly rulers performed human sacrifice, as part of grand displays of religious theatre.

The Pyramid of the Sun, at Teotihuacan, viewed from the Pyramid of the Moon.

# Mogollon culture

The Mogollon culture emerged *c.*200 CE in the largely mountainous area now covered by southwest New Mexico and southeast Arizona, USA. Its people lived in round or oval pit houses with floors set around 25–100 cm (10–40 in) below ground level, accessed by tunnels and made from wattle and daub. They were beginning settled farming, but mostly lived by trapping lizards, rabbits and other small prey in nets, and gathering nuts, seeds and roots.

Over time, they grew maize and hunted larger prey, such as deer, making first more permanent masonry pit houses and then apartment houses of adobe and masonry. Their small villages began to include ceremonial areas called kivas. The associated Mimbres people, a branch of the Mogollon culture who were at their height in *c.*1000–1150, lived on the Mimbres River in southwest New Mexico and are celebrated for their fine pottery. Mogollon culture thrived for more than 1,000 years until, for unknown reasons, their villages were abandoned *c.*1450.

Mogollon cave habitations at Gila Cliff Dwellings National Monument, New Mexico, USA.

# Tikal and the Classic Maya

The Maya civilization was at its height for around 650 years from c.250 CE – an era called 'Classic Maya' by historians. In c.600–900 CE, Tikal in the Petén region of Guatemala (opposite) was a major city, trading centre and ceremonial site. Its population has been estimated at up to 50,000 people over an area of 15.5 km² (6 sq miles). Among its monuments was Pyramid IV, site of the Temple of the Two-Headed Serpent – at the time one of the world's tallest buildings at 65 m (213 ft) high.

The Maya were a warlike people and their religion was bloodthirsty. Priests performed human sacrifice of elite prisoners of war, by the removal of the heart, decapitation or shooting with arrows. But the Classic Maya era also saw the emergence of an advanced culture that produced irrigation schemes, achievements in astronomy and mathematics, magnificent sculpture and exquisite painted vases, as well as a calendar and writing system. In addition to Tikal, other major settlements were at Chichen Itza, Palenque, Uxmal and Copan.

# Tiwanaku

The city of Tiwanaku, situated at an altitude of 3,850 m (12,631 ft) near the southern edge of Lake Titicaca in Bolivia, was capital of a large empire that covered parts of Bolivia, Peru, Chile and Argentina at its height c.500–900 CE. Its surviving ceremonial centre contains the Akapana, a substantial stepped platform/pyramid of earth faced with the volcanic rock andesite on which priests conducted human sacrifice rituals; the Kalasasaya, an enclosure notable for its Gate of the Sun carved with an image of the Doorway God (later known as Viracocha) carrying a staff; and a further enclosure called the Palacio. There are also several enigmatic freestanding stone figures. Its people fished in the lake, caught wild birds and herded llamas. The city depended on a very successful agriculture system. Raised fields were built, separated by irrigation canals that retained the daytime heat to prevent the crops freezing during the cold nights at such high altitude. They collected plants growing in the canals to use as fertilizer and in time even farmed fish in the waters.

# The Toltec

The fiercely militaristic Toltecs took power in central Mexico in c.950 AD and founded the city of Tollan, near Tula around 80 km (50 miles) north of Mexico City. They built an empire that covered the modern state of Hidalgo and the northern part of the Valley of Mexico, settling areas with military garrisons and enforcing the payment of tribute – a system that the Aztecs would later copy. They worshipped Quetzalcoatl as god of the morning and evening star in a temple at the centre of Tollan.

The Toltecs filled their capital with battle carvings: four imposing 4-m (13-ft) tall Toltec warriors line up on the flat top of Pyramid B (opposite). Their craftsmen were also known for carving gruesome stone chacmools – reclining figures with a bowl on their belly in which the heart of a sacrificial human victim would be flung during rituals. The Toltec culture had a major influence over the Maya, spreading the cult of the Feathered Serpent, (worshipped by the Maya as Kukulcan), and the military orders of the Eagle, the Jaguar and the Coyote.

# Maya collapse

The cities of the Southern Maya Lowlands, including Tikal, Copan, Calakmul and Palenque (opposite), were abandoned in the 9th century CE in the unexplained 'Maya collapse'. One by one, the cities stopped recording the names of their rulers and royal battle victories on stelae carved with dates in the Maya Long Count calendar. The laboriously constructed plazas and pyramids were left to the jungle. The last dated inscription in the Tikal region was 889 CE and the final in any Maya settlement was at Tonina in 909 CE.

Historians have long debated the collapse's causes. Overpopulation may have led to environmental damage and – perhaps following an epidemic – populations in the Southern Lowlands area plummeted. The constant warfare between city-states, driven by shortage of resources, made matters worse. Other Maya centres further north, such as Mayapan, Uxmal and Chichen Itza, continued to thrive, but the civilization was brought to its knees by the Spanish invasion and the Maya were subdued by 1546.

# Thule culture

The Arctic coast of northern Alaska was home to the Thule people, hunters of walruses, seals, whales, polar bears, musk oxen and caribou that also caught birds and fish and collected mussels and plants. Their culture had a major influence on later Arctic ways of life and the Thule people were direct biological ancestors of the Inuit, who later occupied the same area. From c.900 CE, the Thule way of life spread eastward over the course of 300 years to central parts of the Arctic and as far as Greenland.

Thule coastal settlements contained houses – sometimes half-underground – made from whale bones, skin and earth. On hunting trips inland they used sleds pulled by dog teams and built temporary snow houses to shelter from the hostile elements. On the sea they used one-man, skin-covered kayaks and larger umiaks. The Thule made lamps and cooking pots from stone and carved whalebone. They were skilled in making small ivory or wooden figures that probably played a role in religious rites.

Underground house, or qarmaq, with whalebone roof supports.

# Inca Empire

The Inca established an empire stretching from northern Ecuador to central Chile in the 15th century, controlling lands in the Andean highlands and along the Pacific coast that were home to around 12 million people. They had no written history and historians are reliant on oral tradition and accounts written by Europeans after the Spanish conquest of 1532. According to tradition, the dynastic founder Manco Capac led the tribe from their place of origin, Paqari-tampu, to Cuzco where, at an altitude of 3,400 m (11,150 ft), they established their capital. Beginning with their fourth emperor, Mayta Capac, the Inca embarked on an aggressive expansion, setting up permanent garrisons and forcing defeated peoples to resettle. The economy was agricultural – they grew maize, potatoes, sweet potatoes, peanuts and tomatoes, and raised llamas, ducks and guinea pigs. Accounts and records were kept in a system of knotted ropes called quipu. They also built a remarkable road network, stretching for over 3,600 km (2,240 miles) and incorporating tunnels and vine suspension bridges.

The Incan citadel of
Machu Picchu, perched on
an Andean mountain ridge
2,430 m (7,970 ft) above
sea level.

# Aztecs

The Mexica, or Aztecs, built an empire in the 15th century in southern and central Mexico, based on their capital Tenochtitlan – now Mexico City. The Aztecs probably originated in northern Mexico and migrated south. In 1325, they founded Tenochtitlan at Lake Texcoco, and the following century formed a triple alliance with Texcoco and Tlacopan, to defeat their rival city-state Tepanec and establish an empire.

Like many other Mesoamerican cultures, they honoured the gods through blood sacrifice. They made wounds in their own bodies and slaughtered prisoners of war, plucking out their hearts in temple rituals. Like the Maya and Zapotecs, the Aztecs followed a complex ritual calendar. They also built ball courts in their temple areas for the game that, perhaps, was understood as an enactment of the cosmic struggle between light and darkness. The Spanish invasion of 1519 brought an end to the ancient world in the Americas. In just two years the emperor, Moctezuma II, was overcome and his empire defeated.

Part of the hand-coloured Codex Fejérváry-Mayer – an Aztec ritual calendar, detailing ceremonies, divination and speculations on the gods and the universe.

# Cycladic culture

Settlers on the Cyclades islands of the southern Aegean established a flourishing culture by *c.*3200 BCE. They lived in small communities, fishing, cultivating wheat, barley, olives and vines, and raising goats, sheep and pigs. Meanwhile, they grew prosperous exporting local obsidian volcanic glass, as well as marble, iron ores, copper and lead.

The Cycladic culture is best known for its carvings of stylized human figures, mostly female, in white marble. Some of these represent musicians, for example a pipe or harp player (opposite), but most depict naked women with their arms folded across the stomach. Found in graves, they may have represented a mother or death goddess. Cycladic craftsmen also made beautifully proportioned bowls, bottles and vases. The islands – a group of more than 200 that includes Naxos, Mykonos, Paros and Ios – were named Cyclades by the Ancient Greeks because they formed a circle (Greek, *kyklos*) around the holy island of Delos, revered as a sanctuary and the site of a shrine to the god Apollo.

# Knossos and
# Minoan culture

The rise of the Minoan civilization on the Mediterranean island of Crete from c.2000 BCE eclipsed the culture of the Cyclades. Its centre was Knossos just inland from Crete's northern coast. Knossos is proposed as the capital of the legendary king Minos (the culture's namesake) and site of his labyrinth, celebrated in the Greek myth of Theseus. The palace at Knossos and similar ones at Phaistos, Malia and Zakros on Crete, were first constructed c.2000 BCE, and then rebuilt after they were destroyed, probably in an earthquake, c.1700 BCE.

Minoan culture was at its height c.1600 BCE. By then, the Minoans were seafarers, trading oil and wine for ivory, copper and other precious substances from Egypt and Cyprus. They developed writing, both hieroglyphs and a still-undeciphered script called Linear A, made beautiful pots – famously the light-on-dark painted Kamares ware – and painted lively frescoes on palace walls featuring goddesses, snakes and sacred bulls. They are known above all for the scenes of ritual bull-leaping in their art.

A bull-leaping fresco from the palace of Knossos

# Mycenaeans

From c.1600 BCE, a warlike Indo-European people migrated into Greece from the north and established a vibrant culture on the mainland and nearby islands. Their centre of power was Mycenae in the eastern Peloponnese but they had other significant settlements at Tiryns, Pylos, Sparta, Thebes and Athens – where they built a fortress on the Acropolis. The Mycenaeans were initially subject to the influence of Minoan Crete, but after c.1400 BCE they dominated the Aegean and may have contributed to the decline of the Minoan civilization. Prospering through war and trade, they lived in 'palace states', under the rule of a powerful king and warrior elite. A typical Mycenaean palace was fortified with walls up to 8 m (26 ft) thick and 13 m (43 ft) tall, and centred on a rectangular hall with a circular hearth beneath a ceiling opening to admit light. Frescoes decorated the apartments, showing battle scenes, bull-leaping and boar hunting. Historians call their writing script Linear B, a development of the Minoans' Linear A. In Homer's *Iliad*, Mycenae was the capital of King Agamemnon.

Gold death mask known as the Mask of Agamemnon.

# Thera eruption

One of the largest volcanic eruptions in recorded history struck the island of Thera (modern Santorini) in the Cyclades, c.1550 BCE, overwhelming the Minoan settlement at Akrotiri. An associated earthquake or tsunami devastated the Crete coast and may have contributed to the decline of the Minoan civilization. Some argue that the eruption led to a 'volcanic winter' – a global cooling caused by atmospheric ash and gases blocking sunlight. This may have also caused a 'yellow fog' linked with the collapse of the Xia Dynasty in China, the devastating rainstorms that hit Egypt during the reign of Ahmose I, and even the 'plagues' of the biblical Book of Exodus.

The exact dates of these various events are disputed, so they can be made to align with the Thera eruption. Another theory identifies the eruption and its possible effect on Minoan Crete as the inspiration of Plato's story of Atlantis – the advanced island civilization that was submerged in the Atlantic Ocean after falling out of divine favour.

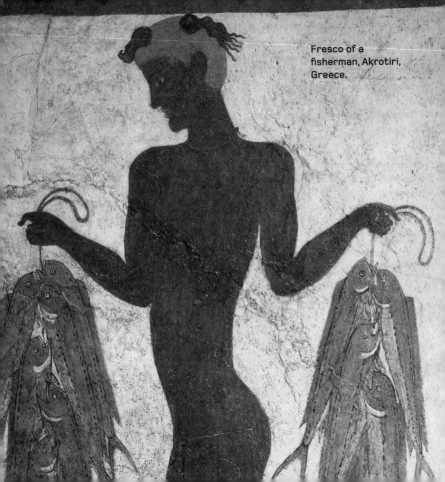

Fresco of a fisherman, Akrotiri, Greece.

# Troy

The legendary war between the Mycenaean Greeks and the people of Troy was a major theme in Ancient Greek literature. Famously, it was the subject of the poet Homer's hugely influential epic *Iliad* (see page 142). Troy was a trading city in Anatolia whose ruins have been excavated at Hisarlik, close to the mouth of the Dardanelles in Turkey. It was probably the place called Wilusa by the Hittites.

According to legend, the Greeks launched the war to bring back Helen, wife of the Spartan king Menelaus, who had been carried off by Paris, son of King Priam of Troy. They laid siege to Troy for ten unsuccessful years, finally entering – and sacking – the city by hiding inside a wooden horse. The Ancient Greeks and Romans were convinced that the events described by Homer were historical and took place at Troy. Macedonian warrior-general Alexander the Great made a pilgrimage there in 334 BCE to offer sacrifices at what he believed were the tombs of the Homeric warriors Achilles and Patroclus.

One of the earliest known renditions of the Trojan Horse on a large earthenware jar found at Mykonos, Greece.

# Dorian invasions

Fighting with an iron slashing sword, the Dorians invaded from the north and northwest and conquered Greece. From c.1100 BCE, they eliminated the remnants of the fading Mycenaean and Minoan civilizations, establishing their base in the southern and eastern Peloponnese, especially at Sparta. The Dorians also moved on to Crete and the southern Aegean islands, including Kos, Rhodes and Melos.

In Greek tradition the Dorians were the sons of Heracles, who had been driven from the Peloponnese into exile in Doris, a region of central Greece, by a Mycenaean lord. After several generations, they returned to reclaim their rightful lands. The Dorian invasion drove Greece into a 'dark age', from which Athens and other city-states emerged (see page 144). However, through their dialect – which survived as one of the dialects of Classical Greek – architecture and lyrics, the Dorians made a significant contribution to Greece's later culture. The chorus in Greek drama was also a Dorian innovation.

A 6th-century BCE decorated cup from the Dorian heartland of Laconia

# Homer and the *Iliad*

Homer is celebrated as a towering genius of the ancient world. We know nothing of him, except that the Ancient Greeks identified him as the author of two epic poems – the *Iliad* and *Odyssey* – both created in the 9th or 8th century BCE. The Ancient Greeks revered these epics as cultural symbols and a source of moral guidance.

The *Iliad* tells the story of the legendary Trojan War between Mycenaean Greeks and Troy (see page 138), dated by the Greeks to c.1250 BCE. The *Odyssey* recounts the adventures of Greek hero Odysseus on his ten-year voyage back from Troy to Ithaca. Legend has it that Homer was blind and lived on Chios. His works were part of an oral tradition in which epics were performed aloud rather than written down. Homer's word for poet – *aoidos*, meaning 'singer' – reflects this custom. Some authorities think he could not actually write himself, but likely dictated the works to an assistant, thus giving final form to poems that had been developed by many.

Achilles tends Patroclus in a Homeric scene depicted on a red-figure vase painting from c.500 BCE.

# Athens

The city-state of Athens emerged, c.800 BCE, as a prosperous trading centre. The previous 200–300 years, following the Dorian invasions, are widely known as the 'dark ages' in Greece because very few historical records survive. They saw the destruction of Mycenae, Pylos and other major sites of the Mycenaean civilization, but Athens – perhaps because of its position – escaped major upheaval.

The city was leader of a union of 12 towns in the Attica region. It had a forbidding citadel on the Acropolis hill with immense 'cyclopean walls' – so thick they suggest they were built by the mythical Cyclopes – constructed in the Mycenaean era. From c.1000 BCE, Athens expanded to the northwest. Its prosperity in this era is obvious in the remains of large vases, some 1.5 m (5 ft) tall with geometric patterns and images of warfare and funerals, found in graves. Athens' position on the sea supported its rise in the next 200 years as a trading city-state, one of several in Greece, the Aegean islands and western Anatolia.

# Sparta

The militaristic state of Sparta was reputedly established in the 9th century BCE. It was under the rule of two non-hereditary kings, who had to arbitrate in periods of conflict, and a peacetime senate of 30 members, who were equals with no differences in wealth. According to ancient accounts, this constitution was set up by the 'lawgiver' Lycurgus, who won the backing of the Oracle of Apollo at Delphi for his reforms. Based on the three Spartan virtues of austerity, military fitness and equality among its citizens, these included a redistribution of property, the banning of gold and silver, the requirement that Spartan men eat together in a common mess hall and the rule that all boys were taken at the age of seven to begin a strict military training. Under this constitution, Sparta neglected the arts and culture and focused on developing a formidable army. This established the state's power over the region of Messenia, in the southwestern Peloponnese, c.800–500 BCE. The Spartan city-state played a major role in Greek history, notably in the Persian Wars and the Peloponnesian War against Athens.

A statue of the Spartan
leader Leonidas,
hero of Thermopylae
(see page 164)

# Olympic Games

The Olympic Games was the most celebrated of Ancient Greek sporting festivals, held every four years at Olympia near the northwestern coast of the Peloponnese peninsula. The other athletic contests were the Pythian Games at Delphi, the Isthmian Games near Corinth, and the Nemean Games at Nemea. At Olympia the games were organized by the city-state of Elis, as part of a religious festival honouring Zeus, king of the gods. Competitors were naked for most events.

The oldest Olympic Games on record were in 776 BCE, when a cook named Coroebus of Elis won the only event, a running race called the stade – a single circuit of a track 192 m (630 ft) long. Other events were added in 720 BCE: a two-lap race, a long-distance race and, later, wrestling, the pentathlon, chariot racing and horse racing. The games were mythologized by the Greeks, who said they had been created by Heracles, son of Zeus, and banned by Roman emperor Theodosius I in 400 CE. The first Olympic Games of the modern era was held in Athens in 1896.

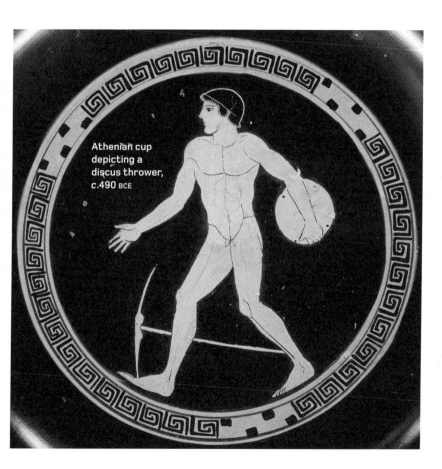

Athenian cup depicting a discus thrower, c.490 BCE

# Solon of Athens

Unrest in Athens between a powerful aristocracy and the rising merchant class led to a crisis in the late 7th century BCE. A land shortage and farming problems saw many poorer farmers reduced to the status of serfs and slaves because of debt. In 621 BCE, the magistrate Draco (from whose name we get the word 'draconian') made severe reforms to try to end the crisis, but they failed to restore order. The more moderate changes brought about by the magistrate, poet and lawgiver Solon (c.640–558 BCE) finally resolved the crisis.

In c.574 BCE, Solon limited the power of the old aristocratic families and introduced government by wealthy citizens. Debt was forgiven and slaves freed; all citizens had the right to attend the general assembly and the right to have their complaint heard in court. His reforms, though initially unpopular, were largely successful and he was revered as one of the Seven Sophoi or Wise Men of Greece – along with philosopher Thales of Miletus and statesman Periander of Corinth.

# Sappho and Greek poetry

A lyric poet from the isle of Lesbos, Sappho (*c.*610–*c.*570 BCE) is celebrated for her poems about women and love. She was leader of a *thiasos*, a community of young women in which members were schooled in the rites of the goddess Aphrodite and the lore of love. Lesbianism played a role in initiation and education. She loved women and may have been bisexual – historians dismiss as legend the classical story that she leapt to her death from the Leucadian Rock because her love for a sailor, Phaon, was unrequited. She is thought to have written around 10,000 lines, although today her work survives only in fragments. The longest – an ode to Aphrodite – is just 28 lines long. Following her death, Sappho was greatly admired in the ancient world. She was included in the canon of work by nine Greek lyric poets – so-called because their work was performed to accompaniment of the lyre – established by scholars in Alexandria in the 3rd/2nd centuries BCE. Others included Alcman of Sparta (7th century BCE), Simonides of Ceos (6th century BCE) and Pindar of Thebes (5th century BCE).

Saphho's poem *On Old Age*, written on papyrus (3rd century BCE).

# Aesop

The author of *Aesop's Fables* – a collection of moral tales, many featuring animals, that deliver lessons on human behaviour – may have been a freed slave from Samos or an adviser to Croesus, king of Lydia. Different traditions about Aesop arose in the ancient world. Aristotle said he was born on the Black Sea coast of Thrace. Roman biographer Plutarch said Aesop insulted the people of Delphi while on a diplomatic mission on behalf of Croesus and, as a result, was condemned to death and hurled from a cliff.

A later tradition established that Aesop was very ugly and an object of ridicule for his appearance. Another legendary account said that he was a black African from Ethiopia, and it is certainly true that some of his stories feature African animals, such as apes, elephants and camels. The fables associated with Aesop may have been part of an oral tradition, although some say a written book of his fables existed in the 5th century BCE, around the time he is thought to have lived.

Aesop, surrounded by animals, lectures an audience.

# Pythagoras of Samos

Reputedly the first man to call himself a philosopher ('lover of wisdom'), Pythagoras of Samos (c.570–490 BCE) was a pioneering mathematician-natural scientist and founder of a religious group. The ideas of the Pythagorean brotherhood influenced Plato, Aristotle and the entire history of mathematics and Western thought. Pythagoras emigrated in c.532 BCE from his native Samos, an island in the eastern Aegean, to southern Italy where he set up a teaching group at Croton (modern Crotone, on the Gulf of Taranto).

He and his followers are credited with working out the first proof of the Pythagorean theorem – that the square of the long side of a right-angled triangle is equal to the areas of the squares of the two shorter sides – but we know that it was used in ancient India and Babylonia. Greek philosopher Xenophanes said Pythagoras believed in reincarnation and claimed he could recall his own past lives. The Pythagoreans developed the idea that numbers were the basis of music and the universe.

# Heraclitus and pre-Socratic philosophy

**G**reek philosopher Heraclitus (*c.*540–*c.*480 BCE) was born in the city of Ephesus (modern Efes, Turkey). He was a leading figure among the group historians call the pre-Socratic philosophers – those who came before Socrates (see page 176). Heraclitus argued that the universe was orderly and opposites, such as hot and cold or good and evil, were connected. A change in one direction was always balanced by a matching change in another. Everything was flowing or changing. Plato famously interpreted this as 'No man steps in the same river twice' – even in the same river, the flowing waters are always different. Heraclitus held that fire was the basic material of the universe. Other pre-Socratic philosophers thought differently: Thales of Miletus argued it was water, Anaximenes said it was air, while the Pythagoreans thought the basic material was numbers. Leucippus and his pupil Democritus were the first to conceive of atoms – the smallest indivisible elements of matter. Democritus' theory was that atoms moving through space (or the Void) collided to form the universe.

Famous for his melancholy temperament, Heraclitus was often referred to as 'the weeping philosopher'.

# Marathon

On the plain of Marathon in Greece in 490 BCE, an Athenian army thwarted Persian king Darius I's attempted invasion. Afterwards, the Greek generals sent a runner bearing news of the victory roughly 40 km (26 miles) back to Athens. The runner is said to have delivered the glad tidings, then died of exhaustion. The event is commemorated in the modern 26-mile marathon.

Darius had launched an invasion of Greece after the city-states of Athens and Eretria backed the Ionian revolt against Persian rule in Anatolia. Athens hastily gathered its army to face the invading troops and asked for support from Sparta – but when the Spartans were delayed, they had to face a Persian force of 25,000 with just 10,000 men plus 1,000 troops from Plataea. Athenian general Miltiades launched a sudden attack, which turned into a rout. According to the Greek historian Herodotus, 6,400 Persians were killed for the loss of only 192 Greeks. The remnant of the Persian force made its way back to their fleet moored in a nearby bay and beat a hasty retreat.

An ancient Greek bust of Miltiades

# Themistocles and Athenian democracy

Themistocles (*c*.524–*c*.460 BCE) was an Athenian general and politician in the early period of the world's first known democracy. Elected archon, or chief magistrate, in 493 BCE, he persuaded Athenians to develop the port of Piraeus and build up their sea power. Themistocles (opposite) commanded the fleet in the defeat of the second Persian invasion of Greece in the naval Battle of Salamis in 480 BCE. Naval power was a key element in the establishment of a maritime empire and the Athenian 'golden age' of 480–404 BCE. The son of a concubine, Themistocles was one of the first non-aristocratic politicians and had the support of poorer Athenians. In Athenian democracy, all male citizens aged over 18 had a right to vote on laws in the Ecclesia (Assembly). The statesman Pericles, celebrated by the historian Thucydides as 'the first citizen' of Athens, helped bring about constitutional reforms and was a great enabler of Athenian democracy. After brief periods of rule by elites during the Peloponnesian War, democracy was once again restored by Eucleides *c*.403 BCE.

# Thermopylae

A Greek army led by Spartans under Leonidas (c.540–480 BCE) made a supremely brave, but ultimately doomed, attempt to block the second Persian invasion of Greece at the Battle of Thermopylae, in August 480 BCE. Ten years after the failure of Darius I's invasion of Greece at Marathon in 490 BCE, his son and successor Xerxes I (519–465 BCE) led an army of 360,000 over boat-bridges across the Dardanelles Strait. The army was supported by a fleet of 700–800 ships. An alliance of Greek city-states, led by Athens and Sparta, set out to halt them in the pass at Thermopylae. For two days the 7,000-strong army held the invaders at bay. However, Xerxes learned of a flanking route and was able to overwhelm the Greeks. The main Greek army retreated, but Leonidas and his 300-man Spartan bodyguard refused to do so and staged a final stand, fighting to the last man. Xerxes sacked Athens but the invasion was driven back when his fleet was defeated by the Athenian fleet in the naval Battle of Salamis. Xerxes returned to Asia and his army followed after the Battle of Plataea in August 479 BCE.

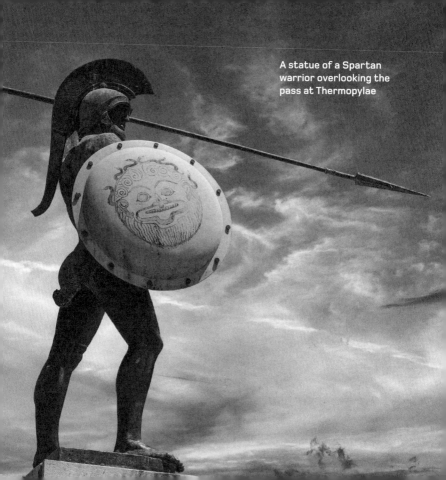

A statue of a Spartan warrior overlooking the pass at Thermopylae

# The Parthenon

The iconic Parthenon temple to the goddess Athena Parthenos ('the Virgin') was built on the Acropolis in Athens commencing 447 BCE under the direction of the statesman Pericles (c.495–429 BCE) and the sculptor Phidias (see page 170). Architects Ictinus and Callicrates took nine years to raise the white marble building. In 438 BCE, Phidias's 12-m (38-ft) ivory and gold statue of Athena was installed and a further six years' decoration of the temple's exterior, which featured a wealth of marble sculptures, was completed in 432 BCE. The temple, measuring 30.89 m (101 ft 4 in) by 69.54 m (228 ft 1 in), was enclosed by a colonnade of eight columns on the east and west, and 17 columns on the longer northern and southern sides. It originally contained a rectangular three-aisled inner chamber that housed the statue of the goddess. The temple replaced an earlier shrine to Athena that had been destroyed in Xerxes's invasion of 480 BCE. Indeed, the Parthenon was raised partly to praise the gods for victory over the Persians, although it was initially used mainly as a treasury.

# Herodotus,
# the Father of History

**G**reek writer Herodotus of Halicarnassus (*c.*484– *c.*420 BCE) was called 'the father of history' by the Roman politician Cicero for his nine-book history of the Greek–Persian wars. This is a key source of information on the conflict that lasted 499–479 BCE, and on the Persian Empire and Egypt of the era.

Probably born in Halicarnassus, a Greek city now in Turkey, Herodotus travelled widely – to Egypt, Syria, Babylon, Macedonia, the Greek islands, up the Hellespont to the Black Sea and as far as the River Danube. He settled in Athens, before moving to Thurii, a Greek colony in southern Italy. Herodotus called his work an 'inquiry' (*historia* in Greek, from which we get the word 'history') and he is celebrated as the first writer to attempt a systematic, unbiased investigation of cause and effect in explaining past events. The *Histories* also contains valuable details on the geography of the empire and traditions about local peoples and their origins. The work was published in Athens *c.*425 BCE, before its author died *c.*420 BCE.

# Phidias and Greek sculpture

In c.430 BCE the peerless Greek sculptor Phidias (c.490–430 BCE) carved a 13-m (42-ft) image of Zeus, king of the gods, that occupied the Temple of Zeus at Olympia. Hailed as one of the Seven Wonders of the Ancient World, this representation of the chief Greek deity had robes made of gold and ivory skin. The god was seated on his throne, holding a sceptre in one hand and an image of Nike, goddess of victory, in the other.

Phidias had already overseen decoration on the Parthenon in Athens. As well as creating a 12-m (38-ft) gold-and-ivory statue of the goddess Athena, he had made or overseen the carving of the sculptures known as the Parthenon, or Elgin, marbles – stones removed to the British Museum in the 1800s. With his contemporaries Polyclitus and Myron, Phidias ushered in the classical period of Greek sculpture. Characterized by graceful, sensuous marble and bronze sculptures of athletes and deities in lifelike and naturalistic poses, this period ran until the works of Lycippos and Praxiteles in the late 4th century BCE.

A reconstruction of Phidias's monumental statue of Zeus at Olympia

# Sophocles and theatre

Sophocles (c.496–406 BCE) was one of the three great tragic dramatists of Athens. The well-educated son of a wealthy armour manufacturer, he was active in public life and served as an executive official in charge of the armed forces at least twice. He entered the city's annual Great Dionysia drama festival, winning 24 out of 30 times. Sophocles wrote 123 plays, but only seven tragedies and a fragment of a satyr play survive – including *Antigone*, *Oedipus the King* and *Oedipus at Colonus*.

Aeschylus (c.525–456 BCE) – reputedly called 'the Father of Tragedy' – was a slightly older contemporary of Sophocles. He wrote the *Oedipus* and *Oresteia* trilogies, and forged the path that later tragedians followed. Euripides (c.484–406 BCE) was the youngest of the three, and seemingly the least successful in the Great Dionysia festival. However, his plays were more down-to-earth and realistic than those of Sophocles or Aeschylus and were revived more often in the ancient world. This is why as many as 18 of his works, including *Medea* and *Electra*, survive.

Greek actors often donned stylized masks, such as this one representing the god Dionysos.

# Peloponnesian War

The great city-states of Athens and Sparta competed for dominance in the Peloponnesian War of 431–404 BCE. The result was defeat for Athens and the eclipse of its empire. The city had been weakened in 429 BCE by the death of its leader Pericles (see page 162) and a devastating plague, coupled with the failure of a bold attempt to capture Syracuse in 415 BCE.

An Athenian, Thucydides (*c.*460–*c.*404 BCE) wrote a detailed eight-volume history of the war that is celebrated as the first work of modern history, in its analysis of detail and attempt at impartiality. It describes the war as far as 411 BCE, but ends abruptly. The author is thought to have died not long after Athens surrendered in 404 BCE – facing starvation under a blockade following the devastating defeat of its navy at the hands of the Spartan fleet commanded by Lysander. Sparta refused to bow to the demands of its allies Corinth and Thebes that Athens should be destroyed and Athenians enslaved, but established its own rule there under the 'Thirty Tyrants'.

Columns of the Erechtheion,
part of the Acropolis
built at the height of the
Peloponessian War

# Socrates, Plato and Aristotle

Three Greek philosophers of the 5th and 4th centuries BCE had an immense influence on the history of Western thought. The life and teachings of Socrates (c. 470–399 BCE) were made immortal in the writings of his pupil and disciple Plato (c. 428–c. 348 BCE), who founded a philosophical academy in Athens at which Aristotle (384–322 BCE) studied. Socrates was famous for his axiom, 'Know thyself'. He believed that wrongdoing arose from ignorance and that people did not desire to do evil. Using the Socratic method (drawing out definitions and assumptions through dialogue), he interrogated Athenian moral concepts, such as courage. Found guilty of corrupting youth and lack of piety, he was executed by drinking hemlock. Plato, known for his theory that worldly things imperfectly reflect eternal ideas or 'forms', had a major influence on the Stoics and Plotinus (c. 204–270 CE). Aristotle wrote on logic, physics, biology and metaphysics. After Plato's death, he left Athens for three years to tutor the young Alexander the Great. On his return, he opened his famous walking, or 'peripatetic school', in the Lyceum.

The influence of Socrates inspired Renaissance artist
Raphael's famous fresco, *The School of Athens*.

# Ephesus

The Temple of Artemis in the Greek city of Ephesus in Anatolia was one of the Seven Wonders of the Ancient World. The original temple was destroyed and a new temple – the Artemision – was built in c.550 BCE by Cretan architect Chersiphron for Croesus, king of Lydia. This version was destroyed once again in 356 BCE by an arsonist named Herostratus and had to be rebuilt, beginning in 323 BCE.

It measured 110x55 m (360x180 ft) and contained a statue of Artemis, the Greek goddess of hunting, wild animals and chastity known to the Ancient Romans as Diana, as well as sculptures by Polyclitus and Phidias. The Artemision was the setting for an annual festival in honour of the goddess. The temple stood on the site of a Bronze Age sanctuary, said by the 4th-century poet Callimachus to have been built by the Amazons. The temple was eventually demolished by the Goths in CE 268. Some parts of it were used to rebuild Constantinople, including the Hagia Sophia (Church of the Holy Wisdom).

Surviving ruins of the Library of Celsus at Ephesus

# Philip II of Macedon

**M**acedonian king and general Philip II of Macedon
(382–336 BCE) unified his own country and then, through
a combination of diplomacy and military might, achieved
control over the whole of Greece. His consolidation of power
and military reforms laid the foundations for the wide-ranging
conquests of his son Alexander the Great (see page 182).
Philip came to the throne in 359 BCE on the death of his
brother Perdiccas III. He reorganized the army, introducing new
training and tactics based on the phalanx infantry formation
and a fearsome new weapon – the sarissa, a pike more than
6 m (20 ft) long. The Macedonian phalanx was professional
and well drilled in its manoeuvres, and helped Philip win a
decisive victory over an Athenian and Theban Greek
coalition at Chaeronea, central Greece, in August 338 BCE.
Alexander fought in this battle at the head of the army's elite
Companions cavalry group. Philip was assassinated in 336 BCE
as he was preparing to conquer Persia, but within six years
his son had achieved what the father had begun.

The remains of Philip II of Macedon were dicovered in a larnax — a small closed box or 'ash-chest' — in Vergina, Greece.

# Alexander the Great

At the head of a highly trained Greek–Macedonian army, Alexander the Great (356–323 BCE) conquered an empire of more than 5 million km² (2 million sq miles), stretching from Greece to the Indian Punjab and as far south as Egypt. It took him just 13 years and enabled the Hellenization, or spread of Ancient Greek ideas and culture, across this area.

The son of Philip II of Macedon, Alexander came to the throne before he was 20, on his father's assassination in 336 BCE. After consolidating his position at home, he humiliated Achaemenid Persia with famous victories at Granicus, Issus and Gaugamela (334–331 BCE), and pressed on to take control of the whole Persian Empire. He founded more than 70 cities, including Alexandria in Egypt, and campaigned to the east as far as India, but a mutiny forced his retreat and he died of fever, aged just 32, in Babylon in June 323 BCE. Even before his death colourful stories were told of his exploits – he was the hero of the Alexander Romance, legends embellished from a Greek epic written in the 2nd century CE.

# Epicurus and Zeno

The Greek thinker Epicurus (341–270 BCE) founded the philosophical school of Epicureanism in Athens in the late 4th century BCE, teaching that simple pleasures are the highest good in life. He argued that humans did not need to fear punishment for their actions because the gods took no interest in them. People should aim for a virtuous life, to avoid pain and find peace of mind. Epicureanism has come to mean following sensual pleasure as the highest good, but this was not Epicurus's teaching.

Around the same time, Zeno of Citium (c.335–c.263 BCE) founded the Stoic school of philosophy in Athens, arguing that people should not struggle against the divine reason that established the rules of the universe, and should aim through being virtuous to achieve equanimity even in adverse circumstances. Followers of the Stoic school in the ancient world included Roman dramatist Seneca, Greek philosopher Epictetus and Roman emperor Marcus Aurelius (see page 388).

An unusual double-
headed bust showing
Epicurus and his disciple
Metrodorus

# Euclid and geometry

Greek mathematician Euclid (*c.*323–285 BCE) wrote the *Elements*, a 13-book mathematical masterpiece focused largely on geometry – the study of shapes, space, points and lines. Euclid taught in Alexandria around 300 BCE under Ptolemy I Soter, and possibly founded its school of mathematics. His geometry has remained in use for more than 2,000 years and is still taught today. When Ptolemy asked if there was an easier way to learn than by study of the *Elements*, Euclid famously proclaimed there was no 'royal road' to geometry.

The book set out to derive geometric principles from basic postulates, such as, 'Any two points can be joined by a single line segment'. His first book includes a proof of the Pythagorean theorem attributed to Pythagoras of Samos (see page 156). Euclid relied on earlier mathematicians, including Hippocrates of Chios, a 5th-century BCE Athenian teacher who collated the first book on geometry (now sadly lost), and the 4th-century BCE Greek mathematician Theudius.

αὐτῇ ἡ ΓΔ, ἄλογος ἄρα ἐστὶν ἡ ΓΔ. ᾧ οὐδὲν ἧσσα τῶν μ̅ πρότερον ἡ καὶ τὴ... τὸ γὰρ ἀπ' οὐδὲν ἧσσα τῶν μ̅ πρό-τερον
παραβληθὲν παραλληλόγραμμον πλάτος ποιεῖ μῆκος
ὡς ἡμμοντος... ὥσπερ οὖν τὸ ΓΔ, ἄλογον ἄρα ἐστὶ τὸ ΓΔ,
ᾧ ἡ δύναμις ἡ αὐτὸ ἄλογος δεῖ. δύνασθω αὐτὸ ἡ ΛΖ· εἰ
μ̅ λόγος ἄρα ἐστὶν ἡ ΔΖ, ᾧ οὐδὲν ἧσσα τῶν πρότερον ἡ αὐ-
τὴ τὸ γὰρ ἀπ' οὐδὲν ἧσσα τῶν πρότερον παραβλη-
τὴν παραλληλό-
μένον πλάτος ποι-
εῖ ὥσπερ τὸ ΓΛ. εἰ
ὥσπερ μῆκος αἱ
ραι ἄπειροι ἄλο-
γοι γίγνονται ᾧ
οὐδὲν αι οὐδὲν
αι τῶν πρότε-
ρον ἡ αὐτή.

προβεβλήσθω... ἡμῖν δέ ζῆται ἐπὶ τῶν τετραγώνων σχημάτων
ἀσύμμετρος ἐστὶν ἡ διάμετρος τῇ πλευρᾷ. μηκός...
ἀπὸ τετραγώνων τὸ ΑΒ, ΓΔ. διάμετρος δὲ αὐτοῦ ἡ ΑΓ·
λέγω ὅτι ἡ ΓΔ ἀσύμμετρός ἐστι τῇ ΔΒ πλευρᾷ. ἀγὰρ
δύνατο μ̅ ... ὅπως σύμμετρος. λέγω ὅτι ἡ σύμμετρος
τῶν αὐτῶν ἀριθμῶν ἀριθμὸν ᾧ καὶ ἐν ἀρ...ον· φ̅ ω
μέρον μέρους ὅπῃ ... ἀπὸ τῆς ΔΓ διπλασίον ἐστὶ
τοῦ ἀπὸ τῆς ΔΒ· ᾧ ὡς οὖν μετρός ἐστιν ἡ ΓΔ τῇ ΔΒ
καὶ ΔΓ ἄρα ἀριθμὸς ἡ ΔΒ. λόγος γὰρ ἔχει... ὅμ· ἀριθμὸς προς
ἀριθμὸν ἔχει τὸ ΔΒ πρότερον ἡ ᾧ ἀπὸ τῶν οἱ ΕΖ

# Colossus of Rhodes

A giant statue of the Greek Sun god Helios guarded Mandraki Harbour in the Greek city of Rhodes, on the island of the same name. In the 3rd century BCE this remarkable monument was celebrated as one of the Seven Wonders of the Ancient World. The statue, 32 m (105 ft) tall, was built of bronze, and reinforced with iron. It took the sculptor Chares of Lindos over 12 years to construct, from c.294 BCE.

The Colossus commemorated the end of a long siege of Rhodes in 305 BCE by Macedonian king Demetrius I Poliorcetes ('The Besieger'). The cost of the statue was met by selling the siege equipment left behind by the Macedonian army. It stood for more than 50 years but was eventually brought low by an earthquake in 226 BCE. In 654 CE, after more than 700 years, the Colossus of Rhodes was broken up and sold for bronze scrap by Arab forces. In the Middle Ages, a tradition that the statue actually straddled the harbour entrance became popular, but historians now dismiss this as physically impossible.

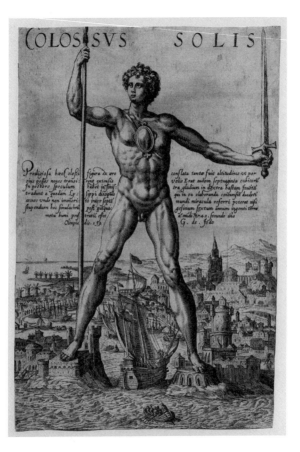

COLOSSVS SOLIS

# Archimedes of Syracuse

Greek mathematician and philosopher Archimedes of Syracuse (*c.* 287– *c.* 212 BCE) is celebrated above all for discovering the principle of flotation – that a floating object displaces a volume of liquid equal to its own volume. He is said to have had the key insight while climbing into his bath – and to have run naked through the streets shouting '*Eureka!*' ('I have found it!').

Born in the Greek city-state of Syracuse in Sicily, Archimedes studied in Alexandria and then returned to his birthplace for the rest of his life. He also developed the hydraulic screw, a device for raising water that is still widely used and known as Archimedes' screw. He designed war machines for the defence of Syracuse when it was besieged by the Romans in 213 BCE. According to one probably invented account, these included a system of mirrors used to ignite enemy ships by focusing the heat of the sun on them. He was killed when the Romans sacked the city after the end of the siege.

# Ptolemy, geographer and astronomer

Greek–Egyptian astronomer and geographer Ptolemy (c. 100–c. 170 CE) developed an Earth-centred model of the universe. Called the Ptolemaic system, it was accepted as definitive until replaced by the Copernican system of Nicolaus Copernicus in the 16th century. Ptolemy proposed his model, in which planets revolved around the Earth on a small circle (epicycle) that itself moved within a larger circle (deferent) and which could predict planetary positions to within one degree, in *Planetary Hypotheses* and the *Almagest* of 150 CE.

Ptolemy is equally celebrated for his eight-volume *Guide to Geography*. This work is immensely valuable to historians since it contains a map of the world as understood by his contemporaries, and a detailed list of longitudes and latitudes for around 8,000 places. Ptolemy based this work on the maps of Marinus of Tyre who lived around 100 CE. We know little of Ptolemy's own life except that he worked in Alexandria, and that he also wrote books on optics and astrology.

# Galen and ancient medicine

**G**reek physician and writer Galen of Pergamum (129–c.216 CE) produced a body of work that formed the basis of medical education for centuries. Born in Pergamum, Anatolia, he studied at Smyrna (modern Izmir, Turkey) and Alexandria, the ancient world's centre of medical knowledge. In 162 CE, Galen settled in Rome, and soon afterwards became physician to Roman emperors including Marcus Aurelius and Septimius Severus. His medical theories were based on his own dissections of animals, including dogs, sheep, pigs and the Barbary macaque, and on earlier knowledge of the body – especially the work of Hippocrates, the 5th/4th century BCE Greek physician who reputedly wrote the Hippocratic Oath. Galen established the difference between arteries and veins, and also that arteries carry blood, not air, as had been previously thought. He produced about 300 works, which were being taught in Alexandria by the 5th/6th century CE. Translated into Arabic and Syriac in the 9th century, and then Latin, they became core texts of the medical curriculum in the universities of the Middle Ages.

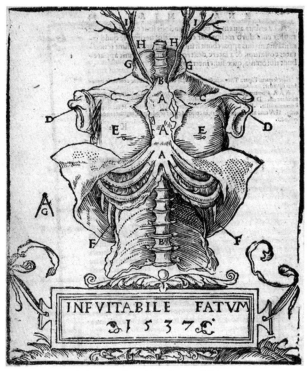

Renaissance scholars such as Mundinus of Bologna struggled to reconcile new discoveries with Galen's ideas.

# Plotinus and Neoplatonism

**G**reek-speaking philosopher Plotinus (c.205–270 CE) founded a school of philosophy influenced by Plato and later called Neoplatonism. He was probably born in Lycopolis in Egypt, and studied in Alexandria and Persia before settling in Rome, c.244 CE. He taught that the source of the universe was a transcendent unity – 'the One' – which was beyond all multiplicity or division. From the One emanated the divine mind or principle or order, sometimes called the Logos; from the Logos emanated the World Soul, meaning the oneness of all living beings; and from the World Soul came human souls and the matter of the physical world.

Plotinus taught that it was possible to achieve a mystical unity with the One – a concept similar to Eastern enlightenment. Neoplatonism had a major influence on centuries of mystical thought, and the development of Judaism, Christianity and Islam. Plotinus' pupil, Porphyry of Tyre, collected his master's teachings in the *Enneads* in the year that Plotinus died in Campania, Italy.

# Harappa

The great Harappan or Indus Valley civilization, based in what is now Pakistan, boasted major cities at Harappa and Mohenjo-daro. Equipped with sturdy citadels, communal granaries, houses laid out in a grid pattern and superbly engineered water supplies and covered brick sewers, these cities were each home to around 30,000 people. At its height, the civilization, which lasted from c.2600 BCE to at least 2000 BCE, covered 1.3 million km² (500,000 square miles), as far west as the Kathiawar peninsula in western India.

From their port at Lothal on the Gulf of Cambay, the Indus people carried out long-distance trade with Egypt and Mesopotamia. They lived by farming, growing wheat and barley, and keeping cattle. Soapstone seals found with carvings of a horned figure in a yogic posture and a single-horned bull may be early forms of the Hindu god Shiva and his sacred bull Nandi. A bitumen-lined bathing tank in a priestly residence at Mohenjo-daro may prefigure the ritual bathing of Hinduism.

The archaeological site of Harappa in Punjab, Pakistan, contains the ruins of a Bronze Age fortified city.

# Rig Veda

The oldest sacred work in Hinduism was composed orally in Sanskrit around 1500 BCE. It contained the hymns and holy poems of the Indo-European migrants (at one time called Aryans), who swept away the already declining Harappan civilization when they invaded the Indus and Ganges valleys. They left their ancestral homeland between the Black and Caspian seas around 500 years earlier, and came to the Indian subcontinent by way of Iran. Archaeological remains show that the nomads overwhelmed Mohenjo-daro, setting fires, cutting down inhabitants and leaving them where they lay. The Harappan civilization was already greatly weakened, perhaps by rising sea levels silting up rivers and causing flooding. The paler-skinned cattle-herders brought with them a pantheon of deities – the lusty war god Indra, the sun and fire god Agni, and Soma, a moon god associated with a hallucinogenic drink used in religious ritual. The *Rig Veda* was passed on by oral tradition until it was written down in c.300 BCE. The book and other *Vedas* or scriptures give their name to the Vedic period (c.1500–600 BCE).

Hindu sculpture of a female nature spirit or *apsara*

# Indian mathematics

The people of Vedic India made advanced mathematical breakthroughs. The first recorded reference to zero came in 876 BCE, an unnamed mathematician proposing the introduction of a symbol to indicate an unused row on an abacus. In *The Sulbasutras* – appendices written *c.*800–200 BCE to the Vedic scriptures, describing the technique for constructing brick altars used in religious sacrifices – there is evidence that the Indians had knowledge of the Pythagorean theorem, as well as how to calculate pi (the ratio of a circle's circumference to its diameter) and the square root of 2.

A Jain cosmological text of *c.*400 BCE divided numbers into three categories: the countable, those beyond counting and the infinite. In *c.*300 BCE, Pingala described the first known binary counting system in a discussion of Sanskrit prosody, using the words *laghu* (light) and *guru* (heavy) in place of 0 and 1. The first actual appearance of the zero symbol we use today was in the *Bakhshali* manuscript, dated in 2017 to the 3rd/4th century CE.

Traditional Indian forms of the digits from 0 to 9

# Magadha and
# other monarchies

**B**ased at Rajagriha, northeastern India, the Magadha monarchy became the dominant force among several kingdoms around 600 BCE. According to the *Mahabharata* epic, Rajagriha (modern Rajgir) was the base for King Jarasandha, leader of the Pauravas. Other kingdoms included Kosala, with its capital at Shravasti and an important base at Ayodhya – in religious tradition and the epic poem the *Ramayana*, the birthplace of Prince Rama. Another was Kashi (now Varanasi) – a centre for ivory, muslin and silk and, reputedly, where Buddhism arose. The Buddha gave his first sermon at Sarnath, just 13 km (8 miles) away.

The power of the Magadha kings derived largely from their position on the Ganges, and their capacity to control trade on the river and access the ports of the Ganges delta. The region of the Magadha kingdom was later the base for larger kingdoms and empires through to the 8th century CE, including under the Nanda, Mauryan and Gupta dynasties.

Stamped and unstamped metal plates – called *karshapana* – were used as currency in the Magadha kingdom, *c.* 350 BCE.

# Buddha

The religious philosophy of Buddhism emerged in northern India in the 6th century BCE, from the life and teachings of Siddhartha Gautama, a member of the *kshatriya* (warrior) caste and a chieftain's son in the Kosala kingdom. Later known as the Buddha ('Enlightened One'), he is said to have abandoned a comfortable palace life at the age of 29 to become a wandering ascetic in search of a way to escape human suffering. After six years' roaming he found enlightenment while meditating under a Bohdi tree – a temple at Bodh Gaya in Bihar today marks the spot. He taught that human life is suffering because people are attached to their desires for profit and pleasure, and bound to be frustrated often. They could escape by finding *nirvana* – the extinction or 'blowing out' of desire, and the end of a cycle of birth, death and rebirth. His followers founded communities of nuns and monks.

The movement was part of a challenge by the *kshatriya* caste to the dominance of the Vedic priests (*brahmins*), and their insistence on the use of elaborate sacrificial rituals.

# Jainism

The ancient religion and philosophy of Jainism developed in eastern India between the 7th and 5th centuries BCE, as part of the reaction against the Vedic reliance on ritual sacrifice that also gave rise to Buddhism. Its name comes from the Sanskrit verb *ji* (to conquer). Jains aim to conquer the senses and passions to achieve enlightenment – a release from the cycle of reincarnation – through a life of asceticism and *ahimsa*, or nonviolence to all creatures.

The earliest known Jain figures are Parshvanatha and Vardhamana Mahavira (*c.*600–528 BCE), who are revered as the 23rd and 24th 'Ford-Makers' of the current historical age – showing the way across the stream of rebirth to enlightenment. In traditional accounts, Mahavira was the son of a warrior chieftain who abandoned court life to become a wandering ascetic, like the Buddha, his possible contemporary. He gathered disciples who founded communities of monks and nuns while, in wider society, lay followers were often merchants.

Relief figure of Parshvanatha at the Digambar Jain Temple, Tamil Nadu, India. The goddess Padmavati protects Parshvanatha from his enemy while he meditates.

# The *Mahabharata*

The world's longest epic poem, the *Mahabharata* runs to nearly 100,000 couplets, making it seven times longer than Homer's *Iliad* and *Odyssey* put together. It tells the story of the struggle for power between two sets of cousins, the Kauravas and the Pandavas. It is said to have been written by the sage Vyasa, who appears in the poem and reputedly dictated it to the elephant-trunked god Ganesha over more than two years. However, it was more likely assembled from mythology, hero stories and philosophy by priests between 300 BCE and 400 CE.

Some of the material included is thought to date back to the beginning of the Vedic period in the mid-2nd millennium BCE. A second epic, the *Ramayana*, tells the story of how Prince Rama, who was revered as a god and an incarnation of Vishnu, rescued his beloved Sita, an incarnation of the goddess Lakshmi, from the demon king Ravana. Though traditionally attributed to a sage named Valmiki, it is actually the cumulative work of several authors between *c.*200 BCE and 200 CE.

Two princes are escorted before a donkey-headed king and his animal court in a scene from the *Mahabharata*.

# Ashoka

Reigning 265–238 BCE, Ashoka was the emperor at the height of the Mauryan Dynasty, ruling an empire covering the entire Indian subcontinent apart from the far south. His predecessor, Chandragupta Maurya (reigned 321–297 BCE), founded the empire. According to tradition, Chandragupta embraced Jainism towards the end of his life and starved to death at Shravanabelagola, southern India. Ashoka renounced violence after his bloody conquest of the Kalinga region of east-central India and embraced Buddhism. His support of the fledgling movement enabled it to expand across India and beyond. Ashoka allowed religious freedom for people of all faiths, but set out to spread *dharma* (the Buddhist notion of the right way to live), issuing edicts and sending 'dharma officers' across the empire to explain the philosophy. He also raised carved pillars with explanations of key doctrines at Buddhist monasteries and notable sites from the life of the Buddha, including the famous lion capital at Sarnath, north-east of Varanasi, the site of Buddha's first sermon.

The so-called 'Diamond Throne' built for Ashoka at Bodh Gaya, the location where Buddha achieved enlightenment

# Menander

Menander I Soter, a king of Bactria in Central Asia, conquered the Punjab and established a great empire in South Asia in the 2nd century BCE. In the process, according to Greek historian Strabo, he 'conquered more tribes than Alexander [the Great]'. He was the greatest of around 30 Indo-Greek kings who ruled in what is now Pakistan and Afghanistan and he led expeditions as far west as the Ganges valley and to the south into Rajasthan.

From his capital at Sagala (modern Sialkot, Pakistan), Menander was a patron of Buddhism and his discussions with the Buddhist sage Nagasena were collected in the *Milinda Panha* of *c.*100 BCE (*Questions of King Milinda*). Several of the kingdom's surviving coins, made from copper and silver, bear the *dharma* wheel, a key Buddhist symbol representing the Noble Eightfold Path taught by the Buddha. According to Greek biographer Plutarch, Menander died on campaign and his physical remains were divided and entombed in stupas in the great cities of his empire.

The reverse of this coin of Menander combines images of Greek gods with the eight-spoked dharma wheel of Buddhist tradition.

# *Bhagavad Gita*

**B**ook Six of the epic poem the *Mahabharata*, probably added in the 1st/2nd century CE, is treated by some Hindus as their most sacred scripture and known as the *Bhagavad Gita* (*Song of the Lord*). Before a climactic battle, the warrior Arjuna is unsure if he should take part in a conflict in which so many must die. His charioteer Krishna, an incarnation of the god Vishnu, tells him he must fulfil his *dharma* (duty) as a member of the warrior caste. But he adds that only the body can die; the immortal soul is either reborn or finds release (*moksha*) from the cycle of birth, death and rebirth.

Krishna then delivers profound teachings about how to live well, offering three paths to *moksha*. One is to act according to your duty, but not be attached to the outcome of what you do. A second is to withdraw from the world, meditate and seek knowledge (*jnana*), the third to develop devotion (*bhakti*) to a form of God. Finally, in a vision, Krishna reveals himself to Arjuna as the lord of all life, shining as bright as a thousand suns.

Arjuna (top right) faces
his enemies the Kauravas

# Kushan Empire

At its height under King Kanishka I *c.*127–140 CE, the Kushan Empire encompassed part of Central Asia, Afghanistan, Pakistan and much of northern India. The Kushans were descendants of the Yuezhi, a Central Asian people who had established themselves in Bactria and northern India in the 2nd century BCE. They played a key role in spreading Mahayana ('Greater Vehicle') Buddhism to Central Asia and China. The Kushans traded far and wide, notably with Rome, and made diplomatic connections with Rome, Han China, Sasanian Persia and the Aksumite Empire of Africa (modern-day Eritrea and Ethiopia). They were tolerant of religious and cultural variety within their empire – surviving gold coins show Buddhist, Hindu, Indo-European/Iranian, Roman and Greek deities and figures. The empire broke up in the 3rd century CE, under pressure from the Sasanians to the west. In the Kushan summer capital at Kapisa (modern Bagram, Afghanistan), the 'Bagram Treasure' of Indian, Chinese, Egyptian, Syrian and Hellenistic artworks was found in the remains of Kaniska's palace.

Relief showing a Kushan ruler from the 2nd or 3rd century CE

# Gupta Dynasty

The Gupta Dynasty, based in the Magadha kingdom of northern India, controlled an empire encompassing northern and sections of western and central India in the 4th to 6th centuries CE. The self-styled 'king of kings', Chandragupta I, reigned 320–330 CE and amassed substantial territory partly through marriage. It was his son and successor, Samudragupta, reigning for 50 years to c.380 CE, who truly established the empire, defeating and removing several rival monarchs and reducing others to the status of client kings.

The Guptas presided over great achievements in astronomy, mathematics, philosophy, art, architecture and literature. The religious practices of modern Hinduism also developed during this period. The dynasty patronized the great 5th-century Sanskrit poet and dramatist Kalidasa, whose works included plays and epic poems, such as *The Recognition of Shakuntala* and *The Birth of the War God*. The empire broke up in the 5th and 6th centuries under attacks by Huns from Mongolia.

Gupta influence reached across Asia, inspiring the architecture of buildings such as the Buddhist temple complex at Borobudur, Indonesia.

# Aryabhata

The works of Indian mathematician and astronomer Aryabhata the Elder in the 5th century CE reveal the great advances made in Indian mathematics. He worked in Kusumapura near the Gupta Dynasty's capital at Pataliputra. A now-lost work on astronomy, the *Aryabhatasiddhanta*, had a major influence in the Islamic world, while a second work, probably written *c.*499, on both mathematics and astronomy, came to be known as the *Aryabhatiya* and is the oldest surviving document to use decimal place-value notation. In it Aryabhata also covered algebra, quadratic equations, plane and solid geometry, calculated pi correct to five digits – and implied that he knew it was an irrational number – and calculated the length of the solar year to 365.3586 days. Later Indian mathematician Brahmagupta (598–*c.*665) described the use of the digit zero in the place-value system and negative numbers in his *Brahma-sphuta-siddhanta* of *c.*628. Islamic mathematicians adapted the Indian numeral system to arrive at what we now call Arabic numerals – 0, 1, 2, 3 and so on.

# Tibet

Tibet was unified in the 7th century under King Srong-brtsan-sgampo (c.617–650), who married Buddhist wives from Nepal and China and established Buddhism in his country. Under their influence, he built the Jokhang Temple in Lhasa – today the most sacred place for Tibetan Buddhism – and installed a Nepalese image of Gautama Buddha there. Tibet's written history begins in his reign, since a Tibetan script was developed from an Indian forerunner at his court. The key texts of Buddhism were translated into this new script.

Srong-brtsan-sgampo expanded and consolidated an empire, which had been established by his father Gnam-ri-srong-brtsan (c.570–c.619), to include Nepal and areas of the Chinese border, and then invaded northern India. In the next century, Buddhism was strengthened in Tibet when King Khri-srong-ide-brtsan (r.755–797) invited Buddhists from China and India, including Indian monk Shantarakshita, abbot of Nalanda in the Magadha kingdom. He founded the first Buddhist monastery in Tibet.

Tibetan devotional statues of Srong–brtsan–sgampo and his wives

# Hinduism

By the 8th century, when the philosopher Shankara promoted the so-called *Advaita Vedanta* approach, many key ideas and practices central to Hinduism had been consolidated. In the Gupta period, the worship of images of gods and goddesses became common. The typical design of Hindu temples was established, with a courtyard and enclosed shrine in the centre housing the deity's image and often a central tower representing Mount Meru – believed to be the home of the gods at the centre of the universe. As Gupta power declined, worship of the Mother Goddess in various forms became popular, as did personal devotion (*bhakti*) to a god or goddess, especially in southern India. *Bhakti* is found as far back as the *Shvetashvatara Upanishad*, a holy book of the 5th/4th century BCE, and was endorsed in the *Bhagavad Gita* (see page 216), but this was a newly fervent and emotional form of personal worship. Shankara, who wrote commentaries on the *Upanishads* and the *Gita*, taught that the multiplicity of the universe is an illusion masking the divine unity or *brahman*.

Detail of the Hindu Shore Temple complex in Tamil Nadu, India

# Erlitou culture

The remains of a city found at Erlitou in northern China's Yellow River valley, part of a major Bronze Age urban and farming culture, may be those of the capital of the Xia Dynasty of kings. Paved roads, royal tombs, bronze foundries, pottery kilns, earth foundations and palace remains were part of a city that at its height in 1900–1600 BCE covered an area around 300 hectares (740 acres).

There were no fewer than eight palaces at Erlitou. The culture of which this mysterious city was probably the capital was the oldest state-level society in China. Elite burials included lacquer, jades and turquoise goods, as well as bronzes. The Erlitou bronzes, the oldest in China, were made for ritual wine drinking. Historical records of the Zhou Dynasty of the first millennium BCE list the Xia as China's first imperial dynasty. However, many historians consider the Xia Dynasty to be legendary; others think the Erlitou remains are those of the succeeding Shang Dynasty.

帝堯放勳其仁如天其知如神就之如日望之如雲

Emperor Yao, one of five mythological emperors whose origins are sometimes traced to the Erlitou culture

# Shang Dynasty

Written history in China began with the Shang Dynasty of Bronze Age kings. Inscriptions and records were cut or written with a brush onto tortoise shell and bone. Remains indicate the kings ruled on the North China Plain, c.1600–1046 BCE. Later Chinese history revered the Shang as sages, for they oversaw not only the invention of writing, but also the development of a detailed and accurate calendar system. They also developed musical instruments, including stone chimes, bamboo pipes, bronze bells and drums, fine ceremonial bronzes, oracle bones, glazed pottery and advanced jade carving. The king ruled through local governors over around 100,000 km$^2$ (39,000 sq miles) of northern China north of the Yangtze River. There was an established warrior aristocracy who fought using bronze weapons and wheeled war chariots, and peasantry whose members lived by farming. Traditionally, the founder of the Shang was said to be Emperor Tang the Great (c.1600 BCE), supposedly a descendant of the mythical Huangdi ('Yellow Emperor'), the patron of Daoism.

The dynastic name *Shang* depicted in evolving forms, from ancient 'oracle bone script' (top left) to modern Chinese (bottom right).

# Western Zhou Dynasty

The Zhou emerged as a subject state of the Shang Empire, but rose up in the mid-11th century BCE to create their own empire. They ruled for more than 800 years, a period traditionally divided into Western Zhou, when the dynasty was largely based in the west, ruling the valleys of the Wei and Yellow rivers, and Eastern Zhou from 771–246 BCE, when their base was moved eastwards into central China.

The first Zhou ruler, Wu, is said to have defeated the last Shang monarch at the Battle of Muye in central Henan in c.1046 BCE. This successful rebellion was justified using the doctrine of *Tianming* ('the Mandate of Heaven') – when a dynasty became corrupt, as the Shang allegedly did, the gods passed their mandate to rule to a new line of kings, an idea that became very important in Chinese history. The Zhou Empire was divided into feudal states, in which the emperor entrusted territory to local lords tasked with overseeing and defending the peasants who worked their land.

文王

King Wen is often regarded as the founder of the Zhou Dynasty, although it was his son Wu who led the revolt against the Shang.

# I Ching

One of the most famous Chinese books in the world, the *Yijing* (*I Ching* or *Book of Changes*) was originally a manual for divination used by Western Zhou sorcerers. Users cast lots – originally yarrow plant stalks – to reveal numbers that translated into one of eight trigrams (three-line units) that formed into one of 64 hexagrams (six-line figures). The trigrams (discovered, according to tradition, on the back of a tortoise by legendary first emperor of China, Fu Xi) and hexagrams were believed to deliver understanding and control of events, and their meaning was explained in the manual.

The *I Ching*'s underlying view of the universe explained reality and change through the interaction of yin and yang (female and male principles). Commentaries were added in the Warring States period (5th – 3rd centuries BCE) and, in the ensuing Han Dynasty, followers of Chinese philosopher Confucius (see page 240) attributed some of the work to their master. The book is considered as one of the *Wujing* ('Five Classics') of Confucianism.

The ancient Chinese character Yi, meaning 'change', is often used to represent the *I Ching*.

# Eastern Zhou Dynasty

From 771 BCE, the focus of the Zhou Dynasty moved eastwards, as they shifted their capital from Shaanxi province to Luoyi (modern Luoyang) in central China, where the Yellow and Luo rivers meet. The Eastern Zhou years are split into the Spring and Autumn periods – from the *Spring and Autumn Annals*, a history of the early Eastern Zhou Dynasty said to have been edited by Confucius – and the Warring States period c.481–221 BCE, when rival Han, Wei and Zhao states struggled for supremacy.

The Eastern Zhou used iron tools and weapons. Their water-control and irrigation schemes, and use of ox-drawn ploughs, brought agricultural efficiency and the population grew. Meanwhile, new roads and canals delivered increased trade. The Eastern Zhou developed Chinese script and enjoyed a great flowering of philosophy and literature. Artisans produced fine lacquerwork, jade ornaments, pottery and bronze. For decoration, artists used representational scenes, for instance horseriding and hunting, for the first time.

An intricate bronze serving vessel or *pu* from the Eastern Zhou period

# Daoism

The *Daodejing* (*Classic of the Way of Virtue*), a key founding document of the Chinese philosophical-religious tradition of Daoism, was reputedly written in the 6th century BCE by a curator of the imperial archives named Laozi (opposite). Dao refers to 'the Way', the natural flow of life and change, and the *Daodejing* proposes that people should aim to achieve *wu wei* ('not acting'). By not interfering with the Way, they allow events to take their natural course. The Way has mystical-religious overtones, since it is said to have existed before heaven and earth. As a philosophy and way of life, Daoism has had a powerful influence on China. Daoists aim generally to adopt a yielding, nonconfrontational attitude, but the tradition also incorporates the worship of the Dao. It was only in the Han Dynasty (206 BCE–220 CE) that the book became the *Daodejing*; before then it was called the *Laozi*. Modern historians suggest that Laozi was a legendary figure and argue that the book had many authors. Other important Daoist texts appeared in the 5th century BCE, including the *Zhaungzi* and the *Liezi*.

# Confucius

The socially conservative teachings of philosopher and political theorist Confucius (551–470 BCE) in the 6th–5th century BCE stressed the importance of order, obedience to authority and profound respect for parents and ancestors. These ideas have shaped China's values and social code for more than 2,500 years.

Confucius was born in relatively modest circumstances but, dedicating himself to learning, he rose to become minister of justice in Lu state. By the time of his death, he had gathered around 3,000 followers. Confucius is traditionally said to have edited or written part of each of the Five Classics that are central to Confucian tradition: the *Shujing* (*History Classic*) on early Chinese history; *Shijing* (*Poetry Classic*) containing ancient Chinese poems; the *Daodejing* (*Classic of the Way of Virtue*); the *Chunqiu* (*Spring and Autumn Annals*), a history of Lu in 722–481 BCE; and the *Liji* (*Book of Rites*), containing guidance on ritual and education.

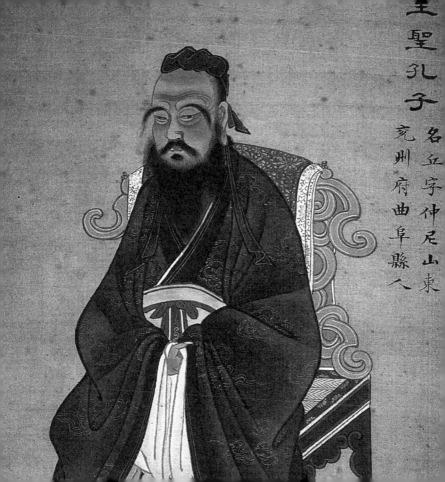

至聖孔子 名丘字仲尼山東
兗州府曲阜縣人

# Warring States

The last era of rule by the Zhou Dynasty in 475–221 BCE is known as the Warring States period, taken from the title of an ancient Chinese history *Zhanguoce* (*Intrigues of the Warring States*). The Zhou kings of the era, ruling as little more than figureheads, were powerless to stop a struggle for supremacy between around seven Chinese states. From this conflict, the Qin emerged as victors in 221 BCE and created a unified empire.

In this period, the main states developed powerful bureaucracies. Battles were won and lost through the deployment of massed infantry. It was a time, too, of philosophical debates. Mencius (*c.*371–*c.*289 BCE) developed Confucian ideas, emphasizing rulers' obligations to provide for their followers and stressing people's essential goodness. He was celebrated as 'the second sage' after Confucius himself. Another Confucian of the period, Xun Kuang, had a darker view in his book *Xunzi* – that 'human nature is detestable', and that ethical rules and penal laws were needed to control people.

The famous Terracotta Army, discovered in the 1970s, guards the tomb of Shi Huangdi, first emperor of a unified China.

# Great Wall of China

The first ruler of the Qin Dynasty and the first emperor of a united China, Shi Huangdi, created the Great Wall of China across his empire's northern boundary, in the decade after 214 BCE. He sent his general, Meng Tian, to oversee the connection of existing sections of wall that had been created by individual kingdoms – some dating back to the 7th century BCE – and garrison this frontier against the threat posed by the Xiongnu nomads from Central Asia.

Where possible, his army of labourers and soldiers used local materials. The resulting barrier was called the *Wan-li Ch'ang-ch'eng* ('10,000-li Long Wall'). Although 2 li measured about a kilometre (0.6 miles), the name was not intended as a measurement so much as a statement that it was exceptionally long. In traditional accounts, it ran for 6,700 km (4,160 miles) from Shanhaiguan in northeastern China. Most of the original is now lost, but 8,850 km (5,500 miles) of a new and longer wall survive, built under the Ming Dynasty in the 14th century CE.

# Han Dynasty

Kings of the Han Dynasty succeeded the short-lived Qin Dynasty in 206 BCE. They ruled for around 400 years, embracing the teachings of Confucius that emphasized moderation, duty and social engagement. Perfecting the administrative structures introduced by the Qin, they split the empire into regions, each governed by centrally appointed officers, and established a salaried civil service with competitive entrance exams and promotion on merit.

The Han era is often divided into two periods – Western Han, covering the years 206 BCE–25 CE, when the capital was at Chang'an (modern Xi'an, Shaanxi province), and Eastern Han with the capital at Luoyang (25–220 CE). The Han oversaw a great flowering of the arts, with exquisite lacquerwork, glazed pottery and fine bronzes inlaid with gold and silver. Screen and silk paintings, and silk weaving, typically showed scenes of clouds and mountains, as well as geometric designs. Buddhism spread from India to China and poetry, history and philosophy blossomed.

Painted statue of a cavalryman and horse, found in the tomb of a Han general

# Paper

In retrospect, the Han years were seen as a golden age of governance and cultural achievement. Paper was just one of many inventions during the period (previously, the Chinese had written on bamboo and silk). Traditional accounts tell of a court official named Ts'ai Lun who, in 105 CE, reported his new invention to the Eastern Han emperor Hedi. He made the substance by breaking down the bark of the mulberry tree and pounding it into a flat sheet. The paper was later improved by adding fragments of fish net, hemp and rags to the pulp.

However, archaeological evidence suggests that paper was made in China under the Han emperors for around 200 years before 105 CE. Knowledge of papermaking spread very slowly to other countries because the Chinese tried to keep it a secret. It passed first to Korea in the 5th century CE and then, via a Korean Buddhist monk, to Japan in 610. Tibet adopted the practice, and by the middle of the 7th century it had spread to India. The process did not reach Europe until the 12th century.

A later Qing–Dynasty depiction of Ts'ai Lun, patron of papermaking

# Korea

Three rival states were established as hereditary royal kingdoms in the Korean Peninsula in the first centuries CE – Koguryo, Silla and Paekche. The largest, Koguryo, was based in the north and gives its name to Korea. It probably came into existence in the 2nd century BCE, although its foundation myth recounts that tribal leader Chu-mong created it near the Tongge river in 37 BCE. Around 200 years later, King T'aejo establshed a hereditary monarchy, and in the 5th century CE the state greatly expanded to incorporate northern Korea, and most of Manchuria and the Liaodong Peninsula in China. It had a centralized bureaucracy and elected prime minister, with strategically deployed military garrisons keeping order.

Silla occupied southeastern and Paekche southwestern Korea; the two allied against Koguryo, until Silla seized Paekche territory. In the 7th century, Silla allied with the Chinese Tang Dynasty and defeated Koguryo to bring the Korean Peninsula under the so-called Unified Silla Dynasty, which ruled from 668 to 935.

Stone reliquary from an early Korean Buddhist temple

# Yamato Japan

The Yamato Dynasty of the current Japanese emperor, Akihito, has ruled the country since the early centuries CE, when it established itself on the Yamato plain on Honshu island as the preeminent among a group of competing clans. The period of early Yamato rule marks the beginning of a unified Japan. The traditional date for its start is *c.*250 CE but this is a matter of debate among modern historians, some of whom place it around a century later.

The Yamato state had diplomatic contact with China and the kingdoms on the Korean Peninsula, and even dispatched an army to fight the kingdom of Paekche in southeastern Korea. Elements of Chinese culture, including ideographic script, Confucian ideas and irrigation expertise came to Japan. The first Yamato era is also known as the Kofun or Tomb period for the large tombs built for its rulers. One such tomb, built at the peak of the early Yamato, was 420 m (1,380 ft) long and contained military offerings such as armour and iron swords.

These late Yamato period sculpted figures were used to adorn a pagoda.

# Tea

By the 3rd century CE, tea-drinking was established in southern China. The physician Hua Tuo stated in his medical text *Shin Lun* of 220 CE that drinking tea improves your thinking. It was an ancient custom – written records suggest the Chinese may have been drinking tea as early as the 10th century BCE. Chinese tradition credits the mythical emperor Shennong with discovering tea in the 28th century BCE after some tea leaves blew into his boiling water. Many historians believe early uses were medicinal only and social tea-drinking came later.

In the 8th century, Chinese author Lu Yu wrote the oldest known text on tea-drinking, *The Classic of Tea*. For him, tea was symbolic of the unity and harmony of the universe. The work discusses the history of tea-drinking and gives guidelines on the perfect way to brew tea. Buddhist monks took the custom of tea-drinking to Japan in the 6th century. The rituals of the Japanese tea ceremony were established by the 9th century.

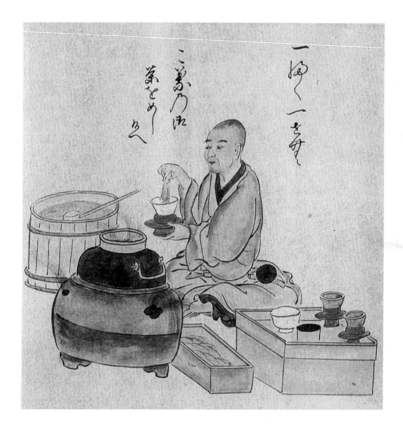

# Spread of Buddhism

Buddhism, which probably spread from India to China under the Han emperors, was a powerful force in China in the early centuries CE. According to tradition, Han emperor Mingdi had a vision of the Buddha in his dreams and sent to India for Buddhist scriptures. Another myth was that Laozi, author of the *Daodejing* and founder of Daoism, was reborn in India as the Buddha. Certainly, early Buddhist teaching in China had magical and supernatural elements that made it accessible to Daoists. It was not uncommon for statues of the Buddha and Laozi to be revered side by side. Under the Sui Dynasty in 581–618, Buddhism became the state religion of China and under the early Tang Dynasty, from 618, enjoyed a golden age. Yet in 845, Tang emperor Wuzong unleashed a terrible persecution, in which 40,000 shrines and more than 4,000 temples were destroyed. From China, Buddhism spread to other countries – in 370 to Korea, where it became the state religion, and in the 6th century to Japan, where it also was established as the state religion in the 8th-century Nara period.

A fresco from the 'Thousand Buddha Caves' in northwest China depicts ethnically diverse Buddhist monks.

# Emperor Wu

Emperor Liu Yu or Wu (363–422) founded the Liu Yu Song Dynasty in southern China. It ruled from 420 until 479 during the Northern and Southern Dynasties, a time of civil war but also a period marked by the growing influence of Buddhism and Daoism, and a flowering of arts and culture. Turmoil followed the Han collapse of in the early 3rd century. The south saw power shift from the Three Kingdoms (220–280) to the Xi Jin (265–317), then the Dong Jin (317–420). In the north, the Sixteen Kingdoms (303–439) saw rule by Turkish, Tibetan and Mongolian incomers. Liu Yu was a brilliant general who regained territory lost to China in the Sixteen Kingdoms period and led a revolt against the Dong Jin. He ruled for just two years before passing the throne to his eldest son. The third Liu Yu ruler, Emperor Wen (reigned 425–453), oversaw a period of relative calm and wealth, remembered as a golden age. Many Liu You rulers were brutal. Ming (r.465–472) had almost all his brothers and nephews killed, and so weakened his empire, and sped its demise. China was reunified under the Sui Dynasty (581–618).

# Shinto

The Japanese indigenous religion of Shinto ('Way of the *kami*', meaning mystical or divine powers) was named to set it apart from Buddhism, which spread to Japan from China in the 6th century. Shinto is an ancient tradition with no founder or holy books, or even set beliefs. It is based on honouring and worshipping *ujigami* – the protector-deities of places and clans.

There were said to be '800 myriads of gods' – the *kami* were beyond counting. Shrines were set up as a home for individual *kami* and a place for them to receive offerings and hear prayers. Ceremonies included offerings in spring and autumn for a good harvest. By the 7th century, Shinto had also developed as a state cult, focused on the *kami* of the Yamato emperor and his family. They established the sun goddess Ameratsu as first among *kami*, and ruled in her name – reputedly descended from her by way of a legendary first emperor, Jimmu Tenno. Observing Shinto rites became a patriotic duty for the Japanese.

Traditional *torii* gate at the Shinto Kasuga Grand Shrine at Nara, Japan

# Zen Buddhism

Zen Buddhism, with roots in the Sanskrit *dhyana*, or meditation, stresses the importance of self-control, meditation and spiritual intuition above ritual or study of doctrine and sutras. This school of Buddhism emphasizes that everyone can achieve awakening or enlightenment under the guidance of a Zen master. It rose to prominence under the Zhou Dynasty empress Wuhou in 8th-century China, who appointed Zen teachers at her court.

By tradition Zen or Chan was founded in China by legendary monk Bodhidharma (opposite) in the 6th century BCE. The name Zen, in fact, comes from the Japanese pronunciation of the Chinese word *Chan*. It became the main strand of Buddhism in state monasteries under the Song emperors in the 10th–13th centuries, and later passed to Korea, Japan and Vietnam. Under the Song, collections of sayings and teachings by 8th- and 9th-century Zen masters, such as Mazu Daoyi and Linji Yixuan, were compiled together with commentaries on them.

# Kyoto and the Golden Age of Japan

Heian-kyo (Kyoto) – meaning 'Capital of Peace and Tranquillity' – was established as the capital of Japan in 794 and gives its name to the Heian period (794–1185). Emperor Kanmu (reigned 737–806) oversaw the construction of the new city, which was based on the design of the Chinese Tang Dynasty capital Chang'an (modern Xi'an). The Yamato emperors of the period were figureheads. The real power behind the throne was in the hands of the Fujiwara clan. It was a golden age of culture with a great flowering of Japanese-language literature and Japanese-style paintings. Classic books include two by female Heain courtiers: *The Tale of the Genji* (*c.*1021) by Murasaki Shikibu, sometimes described as the world's first novel, and *The Pillow Book* (*c.*1002) by Sei Shonagon. *Yamato-e*, paintings of court life and temples, had a profound influence on Japanese art history. The 10th/11th-century Buddhist temple of Byodo-in at Uji is an example of the heights achieved by Heian architects. Its 2.7-m (9-ft) gold-covered Amida Buddha is a statue of Amitabha, icon of Pure Land Buddhism, that was popular in this period.

The celebrated Byodo-in
Buddhist temple at Uji, Kyoto

# Phoenicians

Based in what is now Lebanon, the Phoenicians were sea traders, merchants and colonizers of much of the Mediterranean world, from at least 1500 BCE. They appear to have called themselves Kena'ani and are the Canaanites of the Bible. They built the cities of Tyre, Sidon and Beirut, and founded colonies in Cyprus. In the 9th century BCE, they established the north African power and obdurate opponent of Ancient Rome in the Punic Wars (264–146 BCE), Carthage.

As early as 1500 BCE the Phoenicians had their own script – later put to use by the Greeks, it was the ancestor of our modern Latin alphabet. At various times they were subject to Ancient Egypt and Assyria, and from 539 BCE were part of the Persian Empire. They exported pine and cedar wood, wine, ivory and wood carving, metalwork and cloth. Linen from Tyre was dyed in the celebrated 'Tyrian', or imperial, purple. The Phoenicians were also known for their glass, and the techniques of glassblowing seem to have been first developed in Phoenicia, c.100.

Coffin of a Phoenician woman, discovered at the city of Sidon, Lebanon

# Mitanni

The Mitanni built an empire in northern Mesopotamia that endured for around 140 years from 1500 BCE. They were part of the Indo-European migration that carried the eventual conquerors of the Harappa civilization to India (see page 198), but they stopped and settled in northern Mesopotamia. Their empire stretched from the northern Zagreb Mountains in Iran to the Mediterranean, and was based on the Khabur river in southeast Turkey/Syria. Wassukkani, the capital city, probably stood here, but has not yet been found. The Mitanni clashed with Assyria (see page 40) and Ancient Egypt. In 1500–1450 BCE their ruler Saustatar (reigned c.1500–1450 BCE) overran the Assyrian capital Ashur and looted the royal palace. In the 14th century BCE, the Mitanni made a treaty with Egypt, in which King Suttarna's daughter married Pharaoh Amenhotep III, an event recorded in the Amarna Letters. The Hittites (see page 46) sacked Wassukkani in the reign of Mitannian king Tushratta, and later Assyrian rulers Adad-nirari and Shalmaneser I repeated the insult. Mitanni lands became part of the Assyrian Empire.

This impression from a Mitannian cylinder seal shows various deities supported on bulls and lions.

# Shalmaneser I

Shalmaneser I greatly expanded Assyrian power in his roughly 30-year reign, c.1263–c.1234 BCE. His annals, which have been discovered in the Assyrian capital Ashur, report that he conquered eight countries in the first year of his reign. Furthermore, he reduced a fortress named Arinnu to dust, which he carried home as a symbol of his triumph.

When Shattuara of the Mitanni challenged Assyrian power in alliance with the Hittites, Shalmaneser completely crushed their combined force and sacked the Mitanni capital Wassukkani, before bringing the Mitanni kingdom into the Assyrian Empire. He boasted that he blinded more than 14,000 prisoners of war in one eye. Indeed, Shalmaneser was one of the first Assyrian rulers to carry off prisoners rather than slaughter them. He was also a great builder. At Ashur, he restored a temple and constructed a palace. He also built at Nineveh (modern Mosul in Iraq) and founded the city of Kalakh (now Nimrud in northern Iraq).

This palace relief from Nineveh shows an Assyrian soldier about to behead a prisoner.

# Sea Peoples

Invaders came by sea to attack the Eastern Mediterranean and Ancient Egypt at the end of the Bronze Age c.1200 BCE. Terrorizing the Mediterranean region, they launched invasions of Anatolia, Syria, Phoenicia and Cyprus, as well as Egypt. They are credited with wiping out the Hittites, while ancient Egyptian records refer to battles against the Sea Peoples in the reigns of pharaohs Merneptah (1273–1203 BCE) and Ramses III (c.1198–1166 BCE). Ramses III famously defeated the invaders both in Palestine and the Nile Delta.

Nineteenth-century historians were the first to call these invading migrants 'Sea Peoples'. They are supposed to be Mycenaean Greeks or Anatolian pirates known as Tyrsenoi – the ancestors of the Etruscans of 6th-century BCE Italy. Other theories claim that the Sea Peoples were an Anatolian group, known as Luka, who later gave their name to Lycia, a region of Anatolia in the classical era, Sicilians or even Philistines, a people who came from Crete and settled in Palestine.

Captive 'Peleset' Sea Peoples depicted on the temple of Ramses III at Medinet Habu

# Assyrian Empire

Under Tiglath-Pileser I (1114–1076 BCE) the Assyrian Empire became the leading power in Western Asia. His predecessors Ashur-dan I and Ashur-resh-ishi had built up Assyria after a period of decline, but Tiglath-Pileser's achievements put theirs in the shade. Early in his reign he defeated an invading army of 20,000 Mushki (from Phrygia, west-central Anatolia) in Kumukh on the upper Euphrates, and overcame the Nairi near Lake Van in eastern Anatolia.

Overcoming the semi-nomadic Aramean tribes of northern Syria, he pushed as far as the Mediterranean coast and forced Phoenician trading centres to pay him tribute. After 1100, he defeated northern Babylonia and looted Babylon but did not inflict a decisive defeat on its king, Marduk-nadin-ahhe. Tiglath-Pileser advanced the administration of his empire by improving the education of scribes, and also boosted farming and fruit production. His territorial gains did not last long after his death and, by c.1032, the empire was in full decline.

The winged, human-headed bull called a lamassu was an important protective deity in Assyria.

# King David

The biblical king David reputedly established Jerusalem as capital of a united Israel in c.1000 BCE. According to the Bible, he was a shepherd who became a favourite of Saul, the first ruler of the united kingdom of Israel and Judah, but was forced into exile when his military achievements made Saul jealous. He was then invited to become king on Saul's death in battle, captured Jerusalem from the Jebusites and installed the sacred Ark of the Covenant there.

David crushed the Philistines and captured the kingdoms of Moab, Edom and Ammon (now in Jordan) to create an empire. He was celebrated as a poet and musician, and many of the *Psalms* are attributed to him. In the biblical books of the prophets he is celebrated as the ideal king and ancestor of the Messiah, the Jewish saviour. Some experts say this account is backed by archaeological evidence – a 9th-century BCE stele found at Tel Dan, Israel, refers to the House of David – but others believe David was a tribal leader of an agricultural society.

David displays the head of the defeated Philistine warrior Goliath.

# Solomon

The biblical King Solomon is celebrated for building the First Temple in Jerusalem in 957 BCE and is revered in Islam as a prophet. The son of King David by Bathsheba, wife of the general Uriah, he reputedly led military operations in Syria, established colonies, including Megiddo (modern Tel Megiddo, northern Israel), and a trading empire. In addition to the Temple, he built a palace at Jerusalem and laid out the city walls. There is little archaeological evidence to support the biblical narrative. Some historians point out that Jerusalem's Temple and fortifications date to at least a century later. Solomon was praised for his wisdom – the most famous example perhaps being when he proposed cutting a baby in two to determine which of two women was its mother. The woman who gave way through love for the child proved she was the real mother. Tradition named him a great poet – and the biblical books of *Proverbs* and the *Song of Solomon* are attributed to him – and a lover of women or, at least, a keeper of a great harem. In later secular tradition, he was seen as a magician.

# Urartu

The kingdom of Urartu based in the Armenian highlands rose to become a powerful rival to Assyria in the 9th and 8th centuries BCE. The name Urartu comes from Assyrian sources – its people called the kingdom Biainili. It is sometimes known as the Kingdom of Van, because the Urartu capital, Tushpa, was at modern Van on Lake Van's eastern shore, in Turkey.

From the reign of King Sarduri I (reigned c.840–830 BCE), the Urartians began a determined military expansion, annexing neighbouring territories and driving back Assyrian attacks. At its largest the kingdom reached northward to cover what is now Armenia and southern Georgia; east as far as Tabriz, northwestern Iran; and southwest to eastern Turkey. Its people shared a heritage and similar language with the Hurrians of northern Mesopotamia and were greatly influenced by the Assyrians. Urartu was defeated by Sargon II (reigned 721–705 BCE), one of Assyria's great kings, and overwhelmed finally by the Medes. Their successors in the region were the Armenians.

Head of a bull from Urartu, originally attached to the rim of an enormous cauldron.

# Arabian kingdoms

The kingdom of Saba – known as Sheba in biblical accounts – thrived in the southwestern Arabian peninsula, c.750 BCE. Its capital was Ma'rib, east of Sana'a, Yemen. The Bible claims that the Queen of Sheba visited King Solomon in the 10th century BCE with camels, spices, gold and precious stones. However, historians view this as a later justification of the kingdom of Judah's engagement in Arabian trade.

Saba was one of many Arabian kingdoms in the first millennium BCE that engaged in alliances and intermittent fighting. Others included the kingdom of Awsan, also in Yemen, which was conquered by Saba in the 7th century BCE; the kingdom of Ma'in, in north Yemen, at its height in the 3rd century BCE when it traded in frankincense and myrrh; the Himyarite Kingdom, southwestern Yemen, which also exported incense and was an important staging post in the ivory trade from East Africa; and Hadramaut, in southeastern Yemen and Oman, eventually conquered by Saba in the 3rd century CE.

This votive stone from the Yemen carries a Sabaean dedication to the moon god Almaqah.

# Shalmaneser V and the Lost Tribes of Israel

Assyrian king Shalmaneser V crushed the kingdom of Israel in 722 BCE and drove most of its people into exile in Assyria. Shalmaneser was probably the son of Tiglath-Pileser III (see page 274) and was also known as Ululai. After King Solomon's death, the united kingdom comprising the 12 tribes of Israel – by tradition the direct descendants of the 12 sons of Jacob – had split, with the ten northern tribes founding the northern kingdom of Israel with its capital at Jerusalem (see page 296), and two others establishing Judah in the south.

Shalmaneser V denounced Israel's king Hoshea for plotting with Egypt against Assyria, and as punishment besieged Samaria (part of modern Palestine). The capture and deportation of Israel's population gave rise to the tradition of the Ten Lost Tribes of Israel. Many disparate peoples, including Native Americans, Ethiopian Jews and Japanese have been proposed as descendants of the Lost Tribes. Some claim that the Lost Tribes are those later known as Cimmerians and Scythians.

SALMA NASAR.

# Scythians

Fierce, fast-moving nomadic warriors, famed for their horsemanship and the exquisite gold and turquoise work in their burials, the Scythians built an empire that at its peak stretched from the Carpathian Mountains in central/eastern Europe to China and southern Siberia. They were widely feared as the first people in history to have mastered fighting on horseback and astounded opponents with their speed of movement. They fought with bow and arrows and swords, wearing bronze helmets and chainmail shirts. Migrating from Central Asia towards Ukraine in the 8th/7th centuries BCE, the Scythians swept away the Cimmerians in the Caucasus and the area north of the Black Sea. From bases in Ukraine, southern Russia and the Crimea, they controlled a wide-ranging trade network that connected Greece, Persia and India, as well as China. They were ruled by a hereditary king and chieftains named 'Royal Scyths' who were given lavish burials in *kurgans* (mounds). Some burials included horses, servants and womenfolk sacrificed alongside the dead individual.

A Scythian gold belt buckle from Mingachevir, Azerbaijan

# Ashurbanipal

The last great Assyrian king, Ashurbanipal (reigned c.668–627 BCE), was a major patron of the arts. In the mid-7th century BCE, he assembled a large and carefully catalogued library of cuneiform tablets at Nineveh (modern Mosul, Iraq), more than 20,000 of which are now in the British Museum. The library included scientific works, omen texts describing the divinatory meaning of events and astronomical movements, word lists in Akkadian and Sumerian, prayers and incantations, and Mesopotamian epics, including the *Epic of Gilgamesh* (see page 30). There is even a folk tale later collected into *The Thousand and One Nights*. Ashurbanipal also commissioned superb sculptures and bas-reliefs for his palaces – including the celebrated *Lion Hunt of Ashurbanipal*, also in the British Museum. He was an effective administrator and military leader and overcame a revolt in Babylon and defeated Elam, sacking Susa in 648 BCE. The empire began to disintegrate, however, after his death in 627 BCE. Within two decades an uprising of the Medes and Babylonians brought it to an end in 612 BCE.

A palace relief from Nineveh shows Ashurbanipal involved in the ritualized 'hunt' of captive lions.

# Medes

Cyaxares (reigned 625–585 BCE), king of the Medes of northwestern Iran, allied with King Nabopolassar of Babylon (reigned c.658–605 BCE) and, with the backing of the Scythians and Cimmerians, stormed Nineveh in 612 BCE, effectively bringing down the Assyrian Empire. The Assyrian collapse was confirmed at the Battle of Harran three years later. According to traditions deriving from Greek historian Herodotus, the kingdom of the Medes had been founded just over a century earlier, in c.715 BCE, by Cyaxares's grandfather Deioces. Its capital was at Ecbatana (Hamadan, west-central Iran).

After Harran, the triumphant monarchs shared out Assyrian territories between them. At a stroke, the Medes won an empire incorporating much of Iran, the north of Assyria and some of Armenia. Cyaxares also defeated the kingdoms of Mannai and Urartu at roughly the same time. The empire lasted only until 550 BCE, when Cyrus the Great (see page 298) defeated the Medes and made them part of the Achaemenid Empire.

Decorative vessels called rhytons, often in the shape of animal heads, are among the finest examples of Medean art.

# Hanging Gardens of Babylon

**O**ne of the Seven Wonders of the Ancient World, the Hanging Gardens of Babylon were lush, overhanging terraced or rooftop gardens watered by an ingenious irrigation system. They are said to have been created by Nebuchadnezzar II, ruler of Babylon in *c.*605–561 BCE, for his Median wife, Amytis, because she longed for the green mountain scenery of her country. At this time, the city was capital of the Neo-Babylonian Empire under the Chaldean Dynasty and probably at its most splendid. One theory put forward to explain the seemingly impossible gardens is that they were laid out on the terraced sides of a ziggurat or stepped pyramid. In the early 20th century, German archaeologist Robert Koldewey discovered what could have been the remains of the irrigation system for the gardens in the corner of the palace at Babylon. However, others have proposed that classical sources were confused and that the actual gardens were laid out on an artificial slope by Assyrian king Sennacherib, as part of his extensive building works in Nineveh in the 8th century BCE.

# Zoroaster

Iranian prophet Zoroaster, founder of Zoroastrianism, promoted monotheism – the worship of one God – alongside the concept of dualism, the idea that there is an eternal struggle between the forces of good and evil. His teachings may have influenced the emerging religion of Judaism and Western philosophy through Heraclitus and Pythagoras.

Traditional accounts say he was a near-contemporary of Cyrus the Great and Darius I, and give his dates as 628–551 BCE, but some scholars date the language of the Zoroastrian *gathas* – 17 hymns said to have been written by Zoroaster – as contemporary with the *Rig Veda* (see page 200) and argue he could have lived as far back as 1700 BCE. He taught that a single God, Ahura Mazda, was the creator of all things. But from the beginning, evil had arisen to counter good. God had given the spirits he created free will. The good spirit Spenta Mainyu chose good, and the wicked Angra Mainyu chose evil, giving rise to a kingdom of truth (*asa*) and a kingdom of the lie (*druj*).

# The Jewish exile

In the 6th century BCE, the Jews were driven from Judah into exile in Babylonia. They longed to return, as famously lamented in Psalm 137: 'By the rivers of Babylon, there we sat down, yea, we wept, when we remembered Zion.' Many date the exile to 597 BCE, when King Jehoiachin of Judah was deposed by Babylonian king Nebuchadnezzar II and forced into exile with 10,000 of his people; others to 586 BCE when Nebuchadnezzar destroyed Jerusalem and its temple. The exile ended in 538 BCE, when Cyrus the Great of Persia, after conquering Babylonia, gave the Jews freedom to return home. In exile, the Jews determinedly kept their traditions alive. As another line from Psalm 137 states, 'If I forget thee, O Jerusalem, let my right hand forget her cunning.' Some historians argue that the first Jewish synagogues were established at this time, for the offering of prayers in place of sacrifices in the Jerusalem Temple, and the Torah (the first five books of the Bible and commentary on them) became central to Jewish life. The building of the Second Temple in Jerusalem began in 537 BCE after their return and it was dedicated in 516 BCE.

A Jewish coin from the 2nd century CE commemorates the
First Temple destroyed by Nebuchadnezzar.

# Persian Empire: Cyrus the Great

Cyrus II of Persia (c.600–530 BCE) founded the Achaemenid Empire that, at its greatest extent, ran from Macedonia to northern India and incorporated Ancient Egypt. He defeated Astyages, king of the Medes, in 550 BCE, then took Lydia in 547 BCE, winning control of the Greek city-states in Anatolia that had been Lydian vassals. Then, in 539 BCE, he captured Babylon.

Persian rule was liberal and allowed religious freedom. Cyrus permitted the Jews to return home from their exile in Babylon. The empire takes its name from the dynasty's ancestor Achaemenes, ruler of a vassal state of the Medes, who fought against the Assyrian king Sennacherib in c.680 BCE. For centuries Western historians called Iran 'Persia', after the word used by the ancient Greeks for the empire. It comes from the name of the nomadic Parsa, a people originally from the Asian steppes who migrated into Iran in the 2nd millennium BCE. In 1934, the government in Tehran changed their country's name from Persia to Iran ('land of the Aryans').

# Darius the Great

Darius I (c.550–486 BCE) consolidated and expanded the Achaemenid Empire – already enlarged by Cyrus's son, Cambyses II – and built a new capital at Persepolis in southern Iran. While a devout follower of Zoroaster's teachings, he was a tolerant ruler who allowed his subjects religious freedom. Darius put down revolts, oversaw a number of military gains, including in the Indus Valley, Macedonia and some Aegean islands, and made very effective administrative reforms. The empire was divided into provinces named *satrapies*, each ruled by a provincial governor called a *satrap*. He also built the Royal Road that ran from Persepolis to Sardis, capital of Lydia (now in Turkey), a distance of 2,700 km (1,680 miles). In addition to laying out Persepolis, he built a magnificent new palace at Susa. He was buried in the cliff face at Persepolis that became a dynastic tomb known as Naqsh-i Rustam. Darius is remembered also for his two failed attempts to invade Greece: the first foiled when his fleet was destroyed in a storm in 492 BCE, and the second defeated at the Battle of Marathon in 490 BCE.

# Xerxes

Son and successor to Darius I, Xerxes I (c.519–465 BCE) violently put down unrest in Egypt and Babylon before embarking on a celebrated attempt to invade Greece (see page 164). No effort was spared as two bridges of boats were built to carry his troops across the Hellespont. The first was destroyed in a storm, after which he famously had the waters whipped and the massive structure rebuilt. The invasion began well with victory at Thermopylae, followed by occupation of Attica (central Greece) and the sacking of Athens. But after his fleet was heavily defeated by a Greek navy in the Battle of Salamis, Xerxes was forced to retreat.

He left an army commanded by his brother-in-law Mardonius, but this too withdrew after Mardonius was killed in the Battle of Plataea in 479 BCE. The failure of the Greek expedition is seen by modern historians as the beginning of the decline of the Achaemenid Empire. Xerxes retreated to Susa and Persepolis where he concentrated on palace-building.

Tomb of Xerxes I at Naghsh-e Rostam in modern Iran

# Halicarnassus

The Mausoleum of Halicarnassus, one of the Seven Wonders of the Ancient World, was built to house the body of Mausolus (reigned 377–353 BCE). He was the ruler of Caria, a kingdom in southwestern Anatolia, and part of the Achaemenid Empire. Mausolus had founded the city of Halicarnassus as a new capital for Caria and, after his death, his widow Artemisia II oversaw the design of the monument by the Greek architects Satyros and Pythius, and its decoration with works by sculptors Bryaxis, Leochares, Scopas of Paros and Timotheus.

On a hill overlooking the city, the monument had a large base supporting an elegant temple-like building with 36 slim columns. Above that, a 24-step pyramid-roof bore a statue of Mausolus and Artemisia in a chariot pulled by horses. It was 11.4 m (37 ft 5 in) tall. The building came to ruin, perhaps as a result of an earthquake, but fragments including a 3-m (10-ft) statue, possibly of Mausolus, and a frieze depicting Amazons and Greeks in battle, survived and are today in the British Museum.

# Resurgent Persia

The Persian Empire was conquered by Alexander the Great, who swept aside the armies of Achaemenid king Darius III and torched the capital Persepolis in 330 BCE. After Alexander's death, however, it returned to prominence under Seleucus I Nicator ('Conqueror') and the Seleucid Dynasty he founded. Seleucus was a Macedonian general of Alexander's, who seized power in Mesopotamia, Syria and the greater part of Persia on the youthful warrior's death. At its height the Seleucid Empire, passed on to successors of Seleucus, ran from the southeast Balkans to India. Largely controlled and governed by Greek-speaking Macedonians, the empire was a powerful force for the spread and survival of Greek culture and customs throughout this vast area. Some aspects of Hellenization provoked resistance. For example, the efforts of Antiochus IV (reigned 175–163) to impose Greek religion on the Jews led to the uprising of Judas Maccabeus and, eventually, to the loss of Judaea from the empire. The Seleucid Empire was eventually conquered by Rome in 64 BCE.

Coin of Seleucus I Nicator

# The Parthians

From a base in Iran, the Parthians built an empire in c.247 BCE–226 CE, which at its height extended from the Euphrates to the Indus. They were originally inhabitants of a *satrapy* of the Seleucid Empire in northeastern Iran, but achieved independence under Arsaces I (reigned c.250–211 BCE). His successors, especially Mithradates I (reigned 171–138 BCE), took control of Iran and Mesopotamia, driving the Seleucids into Syria.

Their military expansion was driven by their highly mobile and feared cavalry, who were famous for pretending to retreat, and then firing arrows over their shoulders at pursuing troops. This was an extraordinary feat of horsemanship before the invention of the stirrup, and was celebrated as the 'Parthian shot'. The Parthians grew rich from taxes on merchant trade between Asia and the Mediterranean Sea along the Silk Route. The empire fell away in the first centuries AD but survived until 226 CE, when the final Parthian king, Ardavan, was defeated by Ardashir I, founder of the Sasanian Empire.

Parthian art includes striking frescoes, typically featuring figures that stare directly at the viewer.

# Judas Maccabaeus

**P**riest and guerrilla leader Judas Maccabaeus defeated a succession of armies to foil the attempts of Seleucid king Antiochus IV to impose Greek religion on the Jews. As part of the resistance to Greek rule, he cleansed and rededicated the Jerusalem Temple in 164 BCE – events remembered each year in the Jewish celebration of Hanukkah, the festival of lights. Judas's father Mattathias began the revolt after Antiochus attempted to outlaw Jewish ritual. On his deathbed, he chose Judas as his successor. Judas ambushed and defeated a much larger Seleucid army at Nahal el-Haramiah in 167 BCE, killing Seleucid general Apollonius and seizing his sword, which he used in battle thereafter. This inspirational victory won the rebels many Jewish recruits. Other triumphs followed at Beth Horon and the Battle of Emmaus in 166 BCE. The war continued after the rededication of the Temple and, although Judas was eventually killed in the Battle of Elasa in 160 BCE, his young brothers carried on the fight and the Maccabees finally won independence for Judaea.

# Palestine under Rome

The independent kingdom of Judaea, revived in southern Palestine by the Maccabees, came under Roman control in the 1st century BCE. Herod the Great was the Roman-backed king of Judaea from 37 BCE and of all Palestine from 20 BCE. After his death in 4 BCE, the region was ruled by his descendants or Roman procurators.

Shortly before Herod's death Jesus was born in Bethlehem c.6–4 BCE. By the time he became known as Jesus of Nazareth and started preaching publicly c.27–29 CE, his home of Galilee was ruled by Herod's son Herod Antipas. Judaea had been made a province of the Roman Empire and was ruled by a procurator, Pontius Pilate (governed 26–36 CE). Procurators relied on locals for day-to-day government – in Jerusalem Pontius Pilate ruled through the high priest Caiaphas. Jesus was sentenced and crucified c.30–36 CE. The main sources for the events of his life are the gospels and letters of his apostles, but Roman historians Josephus and Tacitus made independent references to him.

Caesarea Maritima was a coastal city built by Herod the Great, and later capital of Roman Judea.

# Masada and the Jewish Revolt

Following a Jewish uprising against Roman rule in Judaea in 66–70 CE, a Roman army under Vespasian and Titus invaded, captured Jerusalem and razed the Second Temple. In a celebrated act of defiance, a group of rebels held out in the mountain fortress of Masada until 73 CE. The 434-m (1,424-ft) high site was probably first fortified c.140 BCE by Jonathan Maccabaeus, leader of the Maccabean revolt, after the death of his brother Judas (see page 310). It had been developed as a palace-fortress by Herod the Great (reigned 37–4 BCE), then captured by the Zealots – the sect behind the 66 CE revolt. A force of less than 1,000 held the fortress for nearly two years against a 15,000-strong Roman legion 'X Fretensis', commanded by Flavius Silva. Jewish priest and historian Joseph Ben Matthias, known to history as Flavius Josephus, fought in the revolt, and later wrote a seven-book history of the war that is prized by historians – not least for its account of Roman military strategy. In Josephus's account, the defenders of Masada committed suicide rather than surrender to Rome.

# Dead Sea Scrolls

Fragments of chiefly Hebrew manuscripts first discovered in 1947 on the northwest shore of the Dead Sea and dating mainly from the 3rd to the 1st century BCE contain hymns, psalms, versions of books of the Hebrew Bible, lists of Temple treasures and a Temple Scroll describing the ideal Jerusalem Temple. Other finds at associated sites have made it possible for scholars to establish that a stable form of the Hebrew Bible existed by 70 CE. Some of the manuscripts are thought to be the library of the Essenes, an ascetic Jewish religious sect committed to ritual purity, which flourished in the 2nd century BCE to the 1st century CE. The Essenes are thought to have hidden the manuscripts when their community at Qumran, near the Dead Sea, fell to the Roman army in 68 CE. In one cache near Jericho, Aramaic manuscripts were hidden by Samarians who were attacked by troops of Alexander the Great in 331 BCE. Another at Wadi Al-Murabba'at near Qumran turned up Hebrew, Aramaic and Greek documents hidden by rebels during the Second Jewish–Roman war in 132–135 CE.

אשר זב...

עולה לוד

...ערי יגזות שג

...חה ונסבמד נ...

...ער ואחר

...יגול יאחד בב

...ומכה ...מה אשר מעד יעמא

...ד ...מה יאחר עולת זה

...ה ...ד ...ן שוזף חג...

...רי מושעוד נאחריזה ויגבור את עולת פטוה יהודה יבא

בקשא ...וישרפו לפנור את שעיר החזועד לראישוזגה וה...

...דמו לפזבח מבזרק וער ...ימו באאבעו על ארבעקרנות מ...

...חעולה ועל ארבע בנות עזרת חמפזח חזרק אתהדמ עליומו

עזרת חמזבח סטב ואת חלבו וקטור חמזבח זהחלב חמעמחאת

חסרוב ואת אשר על חקרבום ואת וותרת חכבד עם חכליות

...מורעוד ואת חזחלב אשר עלוחמה ואת אשר על חכסלום ויקטור

...חבול על ...זבח עם מנחתו ונסכו אשי ריח ניחוח ליהוה ואת

יאריכיד בי יח

לריו ותנבמן לב

ואחר חעולה ח

...עשוד לעולת דל

ובוום זד

...ועשוד עולת בנ

את עולתריאובן

...ועשוד עולת וש

...ועשוד שלת גא

# The spread of Christianity

Christianity spread from Jerusalem across the Greco-Roman world in the first few centuries CE, teaching that Jesus of Nazareth had risen from the dead after his crucifixion and that through belief in him people could find everlasting life. Jesus's followers called him Jesus Christ from the Greek *Christos*, equivalent to the Hebrew *meshiah*, or Messiah, meaning 'God's anointed'. According to the biblical Acts of the Apostles, they were first called Christians at Antioch. Key figures included Saul of Tarsus, better known as St Paul, a Jew who persecuted Christians but converted after a vision on the road to Damascus. St Paul travelled tirelessly to spread the new faith in 40–50 CE. St Peter (opposite), handpicked by Jesus as the leader of his followers, reputedly settled in Rome and became the first pope or leader of the church. Christians were fiercely persecuted under the Roman Empire, notably by Nero in 64 CE and Diocletian in 303–311 CE. In 313 CE, Constantine the Great decreed the faith should be tolerated and in 380 CE under Theodosius I, it became the empire's state religion.

# Shapur I and Sasanian Persia

Shapur I (died 272 CE) consolidated and extended the Sasanian Empire established by his father Ardashir I (reigned 224–241). This empire swept away the power of the Parthians and took on the might of Ancient Rome to become a major force in Western Asia. The dynasty behind the empire was named after Sasan, an ancestor of Ardashir. Shapur was one of its greatest kings, and fought two wars against the Roman Empire. He inflicted a crushing defeat at Edessa in 260 and captured the Roman emperor Valerian, whom he kept captive for the remainder of Valerian's life. The Sasanian triumph over Rome is memorialized in a carving at the Naqsh-e Rustam necropolis near Persepolis. This era was a golden age in the arts, architecture and learning in Iran – superb metalwork was produced, many scholarly works were translated into Pahlavi and perhaps the dynasty's most famous ruler, Khosrow I (reigned 531–579), built a magnificent palace at Ctesiphon. Zoroastrianism was the religion of the empire, which endured until it was conquered by Bedouin Arabs in 637–651.

This glass cameo depicts Shapur's humiliation of the Emperor Valerian –
one of three Roman emperors he defeated during his campaigns.

# Manichaeism

Manichaeism was founded by Iranian preacher Mani I (c. 216–274) in the Sasanian Empire. It spread east to China and west to the Roman Empire, and became one of the world's most widely dispersed religions and a major competitor to Christianity. Of Parthian heritage, Mani (depicted opposite) was born in southern Babylonia, and began preaching at the age of 24 after he received the second of two revelations. He saw himself as an Apostle of Light who completed the teaching of earlier prophets, including the Buddha, Zoroaster and Jesus with a universal religion for all peoples. Manichaeism was a dualistic religion, teaching that the goodness of spirit or light was opposed to evil matter and darkness. Human souls had become entangled in matter – people who lived an ascetic life would return to light and paradise, but those who embraced things of the flesh would be born again in the material world. St. Augustine was a Manichaean before converting to Christianity in 387. Manichaeism endured in China until the 14th century and influenced a heretical Christian sect, the Cathars, in 12th-century France.

# Mishna and the Jewish diaspora

The Mishna, a record of the oral laws of the Jewish religion, was collected in its final form by Judah ha-Nasi (c.135–c.220), leader of the Sanhedrin council in Jerusalem. It was a portable form of Jewish religious lore that the Jews could carry with them for, after defeating the Jewish revolt in 70–73 CE, the Romans drove the Jews from Palestine. This was the final stage of the Jewish diaspora, the scattering of Jews from Judaea across Asia, Europe and Africa. Earlier stages had followed the conquest of Israel by Assyria in 722 BCE, the settling of many Jews in Egypt and the deporting of the Judaeans to Babylon by Nebuchadnezzar II in 597 and 586 BCE.

In Jewish tradition, the Mishna complements the written laws of the Pentateuch (the first five books of the Hebrew Bible). The laws collected in the Mishna had been passed on orally since the time of Ezra, the Jews' religious leader on their return from Babylonian exile in the 4th century BCE. Together with the Gemara (rabbinical commentaries), they make up the Talmud.

מאימתי קורין את שמע בערבין
משעה שהכהנים נכנסים לאכל
בתרומתן עד סוף האשמורת
הראשונה דברי ר' אליעזר וחכ' או'
עד חצות רבן גמליאל או' עד
שיעלה עמוד השחר
ב
מעשה שבאו בניו מבית המשתה
אמרו לו לא קרינו את שמע אמר
להם אם לא עלה עמוד השחר
מותרין אתם לקרות
ולא זו בלבד אלא כל שאמרו חכמ'
עד חצות מצותן עד שיעלה
עמוד השחר הקטר
חלבים ואברים ואכילת פסחים
מצותן עד שיעלה עמוד השחר
ה כל הנאכלים ליום אחד
מצותן עד שיעלה עמוד השחר
ו אם כן למה אמ' חכמ' עד
חצות אלא להרחיק את האדם
מן העבירה
ג מאימתי קורין
את שמע בשחרית משיכיר בין
תכלת ללבן ר' אליעזר או' בין תכלת
לכרתן עד הנץ החמה ר' יהושע

אומ' עד שלש שעות שכן דרך בני
מלכים לעמוד בשלש שעות הקורא
מכאן ואילך לא הפסיד כאדם שהוא
קורא בתורה ח בית שמי או'
בערב כל אדם יטו ויקרו ובבקר יעמדו
שנ' בשכבך ובקומך בית הלל או' כל אדם
קורין כדרכן שנ' ובלכתך בדרך אם
כן למה נאמ' בשכבך ובקומך אלא
בשעה שדרך בני אדם שוכבים
ובשעה שדרך בני אדם עומדין
ט אמר ר' טרפון אני הייתי בא בדרך
והטיתי לקרות כדברי בית שמי
וסכנתי בעצמי מפני הלסטים אמרו
לי כדיי היית לחוב בעצמך שעברת
על דברי בית הלל
בשחר
מברך שתים לפניה ואחת לאחריה
ובערב מברך שתים לפניה ושתים לאחריה
אחת ארוכה ואחת קצרה מקום שאמרו
להאריך אינו רשיי לקצר לקצר אינו
רשיי להאריך לחתום אינו רשיי שלא
לחתום שלא לחתום אינו רשיי לחתום
מאימתי
בללות אמ' ר' אלעזר בן עזריה הרי אני

# The rise of Islam

**B**edouin Arabs spread the new religion of Islam, founded by the Prophet Muhammad in Arabia in 613–632. Muhammad was born a member of the Quraysh tribe in c.570 in Mecca, Arabia, and began preaching c.613. He established Islam in exile from Mecca in 622–630 at Yathrib (now Medina, in the Hejaz region of Saudi Arabia). In 630, Muhammad returned to Mecca, where he died in 632. He received the revelations collected in the Islamic holy book, the Qur'an, from the Angel Gabriel and taught that there is one God, Allah, who created all things and calls for human worship and submission to His will. Islam means 'submission'; Muslim means 'one who submits'. On Muhammad's death, a follower, Abu Bakr, became *caliph*, or political and spiritual leader of the faithful. His successor, Umar Ibn al-Khattab, oversaw a remarkable campaign against the Persian and Eastern Roman empires, which took Damascus in 635, Ctesiphon in 637, Jerusalem in 638 and Alexandria in 646. Muslim Arabs later spread along north Africa and established a presence in Spain that lasted until 1492.

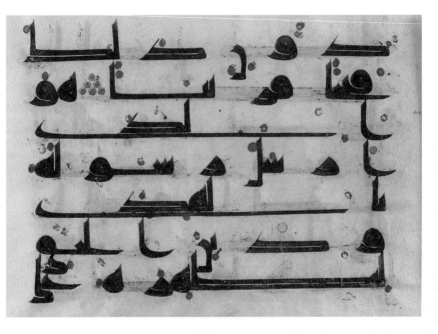

A rare decorated page from an early (8th–9th century) Abbasid Dynasty Qur'an

# Etruscans

The Etruscans were the most powerful people in pre-Roman Italy. They established the urban culture of Etruria in central Italy that, at its height in the middle of the 6th century BCE, extended from the Po Valley southwards as far as Naples and was a major influence on the development of Roman civilization. The Etruscan region was organized as a group of independent towns or city-states and, for a period, Rome was part of Etruria.

The Tarquin Dynasty of Etruscan kings ruled Rome from 616 to 510 BCE and reputedly built the Cloaca Maxima sewer and the Capitoline hill walls. They were driven from Rome in the late 6th century when the Roman republic was founded. The Etruscans practised divination and are known for their metalwork, fine frescoes and breathtaking terracotta portraits, as well as for their building. Their deities Tinia the sky god and the goddesses Uni and Menrva became the Roman divinities Jupiter, Juno and Minerva. An early temple in Rome to these three was established during the Etruscan era.

An Etruscan
silver panel relief
recovered from a
6th-century BCE
tomb near Perugia.

# Foundation of Rome

Rome was founded, according to legend, by the twins Romulus and Remus in 753 BCE, and was established as a republic in 509 BCE. Romulus and Remus were sons of the Roman war god, Mars. Their mother Rhea entrusted them to the River Tiber to save them from Amulius, who had deposed her father Numitor, king of the city of Alba Longa (southeast of modern Rome). The twins floated downriver, were suckled by a fierce she-wolf and raised by a herdsman and his wife. As youths, they killed Amulius, restored Numitor and, at the spot where they had been found, established the city of Rome.

The line of Rome's early kings ended with Tarquinius Superbus ('Tarquin the Proud'). The traditional story is that senators expelled Tarquin after his son Sextus raped a noblewoman, Lucretia. Modern historians think that Tarquin was overthrown by the Etruscan king Porsenna, but before the new king could establish himself, the people of Rome replaced the monarchy with two magistrates named consuls, elected each year.

# Rome dominant in Italy

Rome became the dominant force in Italy in the 5th–3rd centuries BCE. Beginning as one of several states in the Latin League in west-central Italy, the Roman Republic fought Fidenae and the Etruscan city of Veii. Rome was sacked in 390 BCE by Gallic tribes, but recovered to win the Latin War (340–338 BCE) against rival Latin states. The Republic then defeated the Samnites of northern Italy in three wars between 343 BCE and 290 BCE, before winning the Pyrrhic War against Greek city-states in 280–275 BCE. This war takes its name from Pyrrhus (opposite), ruler of the Greek colony of Epirus and commander of the Greek army.

In this period the Republic was governed by two consuls whose main role was as generals of Rome's army. In times of crisis, they were replaced by a dictator for up to six months. The Senate offered advice to the people of Rome. Citizens were organized into centuriate or tribal assemblies, the first voting on military matters, the second on civil concerns. From 451 BCE, Rome had a written law code on bronze tablets on display to all in the Forum.

# Hannibal and the Punic Wars

In the 3rd/2nd centuries BCE Rome faced the north African power of Carthage and its great general Hannibal. The conflict, fought for control of the Mediterranean Sea, had three great phases – the First (264–241 BCE), Second (218–201 BCE) and Third Punic Wars (149–146 BCE) – and ended with Rome entirely destroying Carthage. One of the great military figures of the ancient world, Hannibal was commander-in-chief of the Carthaginian army from 221. He famously led a 90,000-strong army, with at least 37 war elephants, across the Pyrenees from a base at Cartagena in Spain, through southern Gaul, across the river Rhône and through the snowbound Alps – despite being attacked by Gallic tribes. He later defeated the Romans at Lake Trasimene in 217 BCE, and at Cannae the following year, but without substantial reinforcements he did not achieve ultimate victory and withdrew to Africa in 203 BCE. Defeated by Roman general Scipio Africanus at Zama in 202 BCE, he subsequently went into exile but continued to fight against Rome. Finally, at Bithynia in c.183 BCE, he took poison rather than surrender.

# Scipio Africanus

Roman general Publius Cornelius Scipio was dubbed 'Africanus' after defeating the great Carthaginian commander Hannibal at the Battle of Zama (now Tunisia) in 202 BCE. The victory brought the 17-year Second Punic War between Rome and Carthage to an end. One of the ancient world's greatest soldiers, a master of tactics and reformer of the Roman army, Scipio was revered by his contemporaries in Rome. Such was his military reputation, he was seen as the spiritual descendant of Alexander the Great.

Legends grew up around the general – those current in his lifetime included that he was a son of Jupiter, king of the gods, and was favoured by the sea god Neptune. Despite the adulation, Scipio ended his life embittered and exiled from Rome in Campania. His openness to Greek culture, and his magnanimous treatment of Hannibal and Carthage after Zama, won him enemies at home. In the Renaissance, the Italian poet Petrarch revived Scipio's reputation in an epic poem, *Africa*.

# The Italian Social War

Rome's allies in central and southern Italy, known as the *socii*, launched a revolt in 90–89 BCE to back their demand for Roman citizenship for non-Roman Italians who had supported Rome in a number of wars. The uprising, known as the Social War, began after the failure of an attempt in 91 BCE by tribune Marcus Livius Drusus to introduce a law granting citizenship to all Italians. The allies established a confederation called Italia, led by the Samnites and Marsi, and, with an army of more than 100,000, won early victories.

As a result, consul Lucius Julius Caesar – a cousin of Julius Caesar's father – brought forward laws granting citizenship to all communities that had not participated in the revolt, disheartening the rebels. Shortly afterwards, armies under Gnaeus Pompeius Strabo and Lucius Cornelius Sulla won major victories for Rome. Although the Samnites continued to rebel, the Social War was effectively over – though more thanks to Caesar's concessions than to military force.

A coin minted by Sulla during his campaigns depicts his protective gods, Venus and Cupid.

# Spartacus

Thracian-born gladiator Spartacus was leader of a revolt by 90,000 escaped slaves in 73–71 BCE that spread fear across Italy, but was ultimately crushed by the Roman army. His name later became a byword for social revolution, although it is not certain that he and his followers were fighting to abolish slavery or otherwise transform society. Spartacus is thought to have deserted the Roman army and become a bandit before being captured and made a slave. In 73 BCE, he escaped from a training school for gladiators in Capua and made his base on Mount Vesuvius, where many slaves flocked to join him.

The slave army inflicted defeats on Roman troops as they marched northwards. Spartacus was perhaps intending to free his followers in Gaul. They were defeated by eight Roman legions commanded by Marcus Licinius Crassus and Spartacus was killed in the fighting. A second army under Pompey rounded up escaping slaves, and Crassus famously crucified 6,000 of them along the Appian Way that runs from Rome to Brindisi.

Tod des Spartacus. Zeichnung von Hermann Vogel.

Although Roman sources agree that Spartacus died in battle, stories that his body was never identified inspired others to place his fate among the crucified rebels.

# Cicero and the Senate

Statesman and lawyer Marcus Tullius Cicero (106–43 BCE) is celebrated as the greatest of all Roman orators. He tried to maintain the principles of the Roman Republic and preserve the authority of the Senate during the civil war (49–45 BCE) that made Julius Caesar dictator and in the aftermath of Caesar's assassination. The Senate had begun as an advisory body to Rome's early kings and the consuls that replaced them, but it became a powerful government of former magistrates in the last 200 years of the Republic. Cicero became consul in 63 BCE, and foiled the efforts of his rival Catiline to seize power. He oversaw the controversial Senate decision to execute the Catiline conspirators without trial. He condemned the alliance of Caesar, Crassus and Pompey in the First Triumvirate as unconstitutional and afterwards fled Rome, but he was recalled in 57 BCE and wrote *On the Orator* (55 BCE) and *On the Republic* (52 BCE). Following Caesar's assassination, he fell foul of Octavian and Mark Antony, and was killed in 43 BCE. His head and hands were put on display in the Forum.

# Pompey

Pompey the Great (106–48 BCE) was a hugely successful general and politician who allied with Crassus and Julius Caesar in 60 BCE. He originally rose to power through a string of military triumphs. In 83–82 BCE, Pompey defeated the Marians, and during campaigns against them in Africa, was first hailed as Magnus (the Great) by his troops. This victory also won him a Roman triumph – a celebratory parade through Rome in honour of a victorious commander – and he was awarded a second for defeating the slave revolt led by escaped slave-gladiator Spartacus in 71 BCE (see page 340). Pompey was made joint consul with Crassus. In 67–66 BCE he eliminated the threat of the Cilician pirates who had taken control of the Mediterranean and defeated Mithridates VI, king of Pontus in Anatolia. Reorganizing the Eastern Empire, he created an imperial frontier that endured for centuries, and in 61 BCE, was awarded a third triumph. Following the souring of the alliance of Caesar and Crassus, Pompey fought against Caesar in the civil war (49–48 BCE) but was decisively defeated at Pharsalus (near Farsala, Greece) and later assassinated in Egypt.

# Julius Caesar and the Gallic War

A superb general and great orator, Julius Caesar (100–44 BCE) won supreme power in Rome through a combination of military success and political manoeuvring. He was assassinated at the height of his power – a month after being appointed 'dictator for life' – by senators seeking to restore the Republic. In 60 BCE, Caesar had formed an alliance (the First Triumvirate) with leading general Pompey and general and politician Marcus Licinius Crassus, and was elected to the important office of consul. He was given military command in the Roman provinces of Gaul (now France) and ruthlessly conquered the unruly Germanic and Celtic tribes there in 58–50 BCE. While governor of Gaul he twice attempted to invade Britain, in 55 and 54 BCE. In 49 BCE, he opposed Pompey in the Roman civil war, winning a great victory in 48 BCE in the Battle of Pharsalus in Greece. Pompey was murdered in Egypt, but his sons kept fighting. By 45 BCE, Caesar was victorious. Caesar is celebrated as an author for his account of his campaigns in France, *The Gallic Wars*. He also gave his name to the month of July, which was renamed in his lifetime.

# Octavian and the Second Triumvirate

Octavian (63 BCE–14 CE) – later known as Caesar Augustus – was the founder of the Roman Empire, after the end of the Republic in the dictatorship of Julius Caesar. Following the assassination of Caesar in 44 BCE, he gathered an army, defeated Mark Antony and was made consul. Then, in 43 BCE, Octavian made an alliance with Antony and Marcus Aemilius Lepidus. This is known as the Second Triumvirate. With Antony he defeated rivals Brutus and Cassius in the east, and then ousted Lepidus from the alliance; the two remaining triumvirs divided the Roman world between them – Octavian in the west, Antony in the east. Then, in the Battle of Actium in 31 BCE, Octavian defeated Antony and became sole ruler. He termed himself *princeps* (first citizen) and his rule is known as the principate, but he is seen as the first Roman emperor. His was a period of imperial expansion and initiated the celebrated *Pax Romana* – Roman peace across the empire for around 200 years. The 'Augustan age' was one of great literary achievement in the works of Virgil, Livy and Horace.

# Mark Antony and Cleopatra

Mark Antony (83–30 BCE) – part-ruler of the Roman Empire in the Second Triumvirate with Octavian and Lepidus – made a political and love match with Cleopatra, Queen of Ptolemaic Egypt, but was decisively defeated by Octavian (see page 348). His efforts to reorganize the Eastern Empire under the Second Triumvirate had brought him into contact with Cleopatra and they had became lovers in Alexandria in 41–40 BCE. Although ancient authors and Shakespeare made much of their great love, they did not see each other for more than three years while Antony married Octavian's sister Octavia. When Antony returned to Cleopatra in 34 BCE, he staged a triumphal procession and lavish ceremonies celebrating her rule, handed titles to their children and divorced Octavia. Octavian undermined Antony in Rome and declared war against Cleopatra. In the naval Battle of Actium off western Greece in 31 BCE, Octavian's admiral Agrippa defeated Mark Antony's fleet and Cleopatra fled to Alexandria. Antony followed her and killed himself. Shortly afterwards she, too, committed suicide.

Antony and Cleopatra's reputation as doomed lovers has ensured them a long afterlife in Western art.

# The Imperial Army

Rome's first emperor, Augustus, created a professional standing army of 25 legions of 5,000 heavy infantry. The army had been previously comprised of volunteers and conscripts, but in the reorganized military, legionaries made their own decision to serve a fixed term of 25 years. The legionaries wore the celebrated *lorica segmentata* armour of metal strips attached to leather straps. They fought with the pilum, a 7-ft (2-m) javelin, and the *gladius*, a 50-cm (20-in) short sword.

Augustus also created the *auxilia*, consisting of inhabitants of the empire who were not civilians – most of the non-infantry troops, such as cavalry, archers and light infantry, were auxiliaries. Organized in 250 regiments of 500, they served a fixed term of 25 years, at the end of which they were granted Roman citizenship. There was also an elite 5,000-strong Praetorian Guard to protect the emperor, serving 16 rather than 25 years and paid three times as much as legionaries. At the end of Augustus's rule the army was 255,000 strong.

# The Forum

The Roman Forum, a rectangular plaza that developed over hundreds of years as the centre of public life in Rome, underwent major development in 29 BCE, when Octavian finished building the Temple of the Divine Julius Caesar and raised the Arch of Augustus to mark his victory in the Battle of Actium. In the valley between the Palatine and Capitoline hills, the forum had been used by Romans since the 8th century BCE. It was a venue for speeches, elections, trials, triumphal processions, religious activity and gladiatorial combat – as well as having shops and an open-air market. Among the celebrated events that took place there was Mark Antony's funeral speech for Julius Caesar. Surviving structures include the white marble triumphal arch of Septimius Severus, dedicated in 203 CE, which celebrated victories over the Parthians, and the Temple of Saturn, which was originally erected in 497 BCE although the surviving ruins (opposite) date to its rebuilding in the 3rd century CE. The last major addition to the forum was the Basilica of Maxentius, built in 312 CE by Constantine the Great.

# Virgil

Widely regarded as the greatest Roman poet, Virgil (full name, Publius Virgilius Maro) was author of the Latin epic the *Aeneid*. The 12-book poem was a celebration of the adventures of Aeneas, hero of Troy and legendary founder of Rome. Begun *c.*30 BCE and unfinished on Virgil's death 11 years later, it proclaims Rome's glorious, historically validated destiny to rule and bring civilization to the world.

Virgil was a farmer's son from northern Italy, who had a good education in philosophy and rhetoric after coming to Rome in *c.*41 BCE. He also wrote the *Eclogues* (42–37 BCE), a collection of pastoral poems, and the *Georgics* (37–30 BCE), a four-book series on agricultural life. He was a contemporary or near-contemporary of several major authors of the Augustan age, including the great lyric poet Horace (65–8 BCE), author of the *Satires* and the *Odes*, Ovid (43–17 BCE), author of *Ars amatoria* and *Metamorphoses*, and Livy (59 BCE–17 CE), author of an influential 142-book history of Rome, *Books from the Foundation of the City*.

TITYRE TU PATULAE RECUBANS SUB TEGMINE FAGI
SILVESTREM TENUI MUSAM MEDITARIS AVENA
NOS PATRIAE FINIS ET DULCIA LINQUIMUS ARVA
NOS PATRIAM FUGIMUS TU TITYRE LENTUS IN UMBRA
FORMOSAM RESONARE DOCES AMARYLLIDA SILVAS
O MELIBOEE DEUS NOBIS HAEC OTIA FECIT
NAMQUE ERIT ILLE MIHI SEMPER DEUS ILLIUS ARAM
SAEPE TENER NOSTRIS AB OVILIBUS IMBUET AGNUS
ILLE MEAS ERRARE BOVES UT CERNIS ET IPSE

The opening lines of Virgil's *Eclogues*, depicted in a 5th-century manuscript copy.

# The Pantheon

Begun in 27 BCE by Roman statesman Marcus Vipsanius Agrippa, the Pantheon temple in Rome was rebuilt as a vast, domed structure by Emperor Hadrian in 118–128 CE. A few alterations were made under emperors Septimius Severus and Caracalla in the 3rd century. It was originally a temple to the Ancient Roman gods, but was rededicated as a place of Christian worship in 609 CE. With minor additions, architecturally it remains to this day as it was in the 3rd century: a circular building of brick-faced concrete beneath a 43-m (141-ft) diameter and 22-m (71-ft) high concrete dome. Behind the front porch, with its triangular pediment and granite Corinthian columns, are 7-m (23-ft) tall double doors made of bronze. The dome's interior is lit by an 8-m (26-ft) 'oculus' or opening. An inscription on the front reads, 'Marcus Agrippa, son of Lucius, made this building when consul for the third time', but tests have proved that only this section survives from the original building. Historians believe that Hadrian deliberately reused the original inscription.

# Tiberius

Tiberius Caesar Augustus (42 BCE–37 CE) was the second Roman emperor. The adopted son of Augustus, he was famous above all for the 'reign of terror' he conducted while in exile on Capri during the last decade of his rule. Before becoming emperor, he had early military successes but became disillusioned after, first, his brother died and then he was forced to divorce his beloved wife, Vipsania, and wed Augustus's daughter, the promiscuous Julia. The early years of his reign were relatively quiet, but following the death of his son, he settled on the island of Capri in 26 CE and never returned to Rome. Tiberius lived in great luxury, presiding over child cruelty, brutal torture and executions on false charges. He is said to have had a monstrous appearance, his skin disfigured by infections. His mind turned to his successor and he chose a great-grandson of Augustus to be emperor – Gaius Caesar, nicknamed Caligula (Little Boot). In 37 CE, Tiberius fell into a coma and Caligula was proclaimed emperor with the help of the Praetorian Guard. When Tiberius recovered, the commander of the Guard, Macro, suffocated him.

# Caligula

Gaius Caesar Germanicus (12–41 CE) – known by the nickname Caligula (Little Boot), given him by soldiers serving his father Germanicus – succeeded Tiberius as Roman emperor and ruled for nearly four years, 37–41 CE. He is widely remembered as a tyrant prone to bouts of crazed, self-aggrandizing behaviour, but it is difficult to be sure how many of the tales told about him by ancient historians are true. We do know that one of the most famous – making his horse Incitatus a consul – is false.

Some historians think Caligula became deranged after an illness. He is accused of incestuous relations with his sisters, casting himself as a god and ordering that his statue be raised in the Temple in Jerusalem. After his sister died in 38 CE, Caligula demanded she be honoured as the goddess Diva Drusilla. He also marched the army to the shores opposite Britain, in readiness for invasion, then commanded his soldiers to gather seashells. The people grew tired of the craziness and Caligula was murdered in 41 CE by the tribune of the Praetorian Guard, Cassius Chaerea.

# Claudius

Under Claudius (10 BCE–54 CE), Rome made Britain a province of the empire and extended its holdings in North Africa. The fifth Roman emperor, Claudius was discovered hiding in the imperial palace and made ruler by the Praetorian Guard after they had murdered his nephew Caligula. He faced challenges from the Senate, but established himself with the support of the army. He was an unprepossessing figure, who is said to have suffered from tremors, a bad limp and foaming at the mouth. However, he had a keen intellect and wrote histories of the Roman Republic, the Etruscans and Carthage that were admired by contemporaries but are sadly lost. His administration was largely a success. In 41–42 CE, he ordered the seizing of lands in what is now Morocco and Algeria to create the provinces of Caesariensis and Tingitana, and in 43 CE personally led the invasion of Britain. He established the colonies in Camulodunum (Colchester) and Colonia Agrippinensis (Cologne, Germany), and also made Judaea an imperial province. In 48 CE, he divorced his wife and married his niece Agrippina, who poisoned him in 54 CE.

# Rome invades Britain

The Roman army invaded Britain in 43 CE, defeated the troublesome Catuvellauni tribe and established the new province of Britannia, which would remain under Roman rule until 410 CE. The invasion was nominally launched in response to an appeal for help from a Roman ally, Verica, king of the Atrebates, who had been driven from power by the Catuvellauni, but Emperor Claudius was keen to expand the boundaries of the empire.

General Aulus Plautius led four legions and around 20,000 auxiliaries across the Channel. They landed near Richborough in Kent and defeated the Catuvellauni under Caratacus and Togodumnus in two battles. At the Thames river, Plautius stopped to await Claudius, who arrived with elephants and artillery and led the final assault on the Catuvellauni capital Camulodunum (modern Colchester). A Roman colony of veterans was set up at Camulodunum, with a temple in honour of Claudius, as capital of the new Roman province.

A defeated Caratacus was taken to Rome as a captive for display and eventual execution. But a stirring speech to the Senate impressed the Emperor Claudius so much that he was allowed to go free.

# Nero

Nero Claudius Caesar (37–68 CE), Roman emperor in 54–68 CE, is famous for his debauchery and lyre playing, his responsibility for the Great Fire of Rome in 64 and his attempt to blame the fire on members of the Christian sect. This opened the way to persecution of Christians and he became identified with the Antichrist of Christian tradition. He was carried to power by the raw ambition of his mother Agrippina (see page 364) who married the previous emperor, her uncle Claudius, and prevailed on him to favour Nero rather than his own son Britannicus. Then she poisoned both Claudius and Britannicus to make Nero emperor at the age of 16. To begin with, he ruled well, advised by Agrippina, his ex-tutor the philosopher Seneca and Burrus, prefect of the Praetorian Guard. But after he had engineered Agrippina's murder in 59 CE, he dedicated himself to playing the lyre, acting, chariot racing and sex. Corruption spread. In the late 60s CE, facing revolts in the empire, the Senate condemned him, the Praetorian Guard abandoned him and Nero committed suicide.

# Revolts against Rome

Queen of the Iceni tribe in Norfolk, Boudicca led a major uprising against Roman rule in Britain in 60–61 CE. On the death, in 60 CE, of her husband Prasutagus, the Romans annexed the kingdom of the Iceni and humiliated her. Boudicca took advantage of the absence of governor Suetonius Paulinus, who had embarked on a campaign in Wales against the Druids, to raise an army that sacked Camulodunum (Colchester), Verulamium (St Albans) and the market of Londinium (London). Roman historian Tacitus (see page 378) reported that Boudicca and the rebels massacred 70,000 and inflicted a devastating defeat on the 9th Legion. However, when Paulinus returned, he won a great victory in the Battle of Watling Street.

When a second major revolt erupted in Judaea in 66 CE, the future emperor Vespasian and his son Titus were ruthless. They invaded, besieged and took Jerusalem, in 70, burning the city and the Second Temple to the ground. It took until 73 CE to stamp out the last resistance at Masada (see page 314).

# Vespasian

Titus Flavius Vespasianus (9–79 CE) restored order in July 69 CE, following a civil war that erupted after Nero's suicide. He ruled for ten years and established a Flavian Dynasty that held power through his sons Titus and Domitian until 96 CE. His reign began with the so-called Year of the Four Emperors, in which Galba, Otho, Vitellius and Vespasian himself claimed power in succession. After the rapid rise and fall of Galba and Otho, Vespasian was declared emperor by the legions in Egypt, Syria and Judaea, and prevailed over Vitellius to claim power. He reformed imperial finances, improved army discipline and embarked on major building works in Rome – not least the vast Flavian Amphitheatre, better known as the Colosseum (see page 376).

Before becoming emperor, Vespasian had proved himself a very successful general in the invasion of Britain in 43 CE. He won triumphal honours, became a consul in 51 CE. and was later involved in the suppression of the Jewish Revolt (see page 314). On his death in 79 CE, he was acclaimed a god.

# The eruption of Vesuvius

One of the most famous events of Ancient Roman history was a natural disaster – the violent eruption on August 24–25, 79 CE of Mount Vesuvius, a volcano beside the Bay of Naples in southern Italy. The eruption occurred very suddenly but then continued for two days, and the ash flow buried Pompeii, Stabiae, Torre Annunziata and Herculaneum. Lawyer and author Pliny the Younger (61–c.113 CE) was staying nearby and famously described the events in two letters to the historian Tacitus (see page 378). The volcano's deadly hot ash preserved the places it buried, capturing them for posterity as they were on the day of the eruption. More than 1,000 casts have been made of human bodies caught in the ashes in Pompeii and more than 300 have been made in Herculaneum. Private homes with domestic shrines, beautiful wall paintings, furniture and mosaics have been restored. More modest homes and workspaces like bakeries and fulleries (wool laundries) have also been discovered. Pompeii's ruins were found in the late 16th century, but excavations didn't begin until 1748.

# The Colosseum

Ancient Rome's most iconic site is the Colosseum, a giant freestanding amphitheatre in which crowds of 50,000 enthusiastically watched martial encounters including mock naval battles and gladiatorial fights to the death. At one time historians suggested that early Christians were forced to fight wild animals before bloodthirsty crowds, and many were martyred, but experts now doubt whether this happened. The Colosseum was begun by Vespasian in CE 70–72 on the site of an artificial lake that was part of Emperor Nero's palace. Titus dedicated it in CE 80, with a 100-day festival of games. Two years later, Domitian added a further storey.

Measuring 189x156 m (620x512 ft), the three-storey stone and concrete Colosseum is the largest amphitheatre ever built. Some of the 100,000 Jewish prisoners brought to Rome after the Siege of Jerusalem worked on the construction, which was funded by the spoils of war. The building was long neglected, but attempts to preserve it began in the 19th century.

The Colosseum is thought
to have been named from an
adjacent bronze statue, the
Colossus of Nero, that survived
into medieval times.

# Tacitus

The superbly written works of senator and historian Publius Cornelius Tacitus (c.56–120 CE) are a key source for the history of Rome in the 1st century CE. They include the *Annals* and *Histories*, which cover Rome from the death of Augustus in 14 CE to 96 CE, a history of the Germanic tribes in *Germania* and a life of his father-in-law, the Roman general Agricola, that gives a vivid account of Agricola's time as governor of Britain in 77–85 CE. Tacitus is widely praised for his concise, penetrating prose style in Latin, which experts liken to that of earlier Roman historian Sallust (86–34 BCE) and contrast with the more sonorous Latin of Cicero (see page 342). Born probably in northern Italy or southern France, he studied rhetoric in Rome and won a great reputation as an orator. His marriage to Agricola's daughter Julia helped him rise to prominence: he became quaestor, praetor and finally consul in 97 CE. He was friends with Pliny the Younger and, together in 100 CE, they successfully prosecuted the proconsul of Africa, Marius Priscus, who had been accused of corruption.

# Mithraism

The pre-Zoroastrian Iranian religion of Mithraism enjoyed a wave of popularity in the Roman Empire in the 2nd and 3rd centuries CE, notably among soldiers. Legionaries worshipped Mithras – originally, the Iranian god of the sun, justice and war. The Roman form of the religion focused on loyalty to the emperor – emperors from Commodus to Caracalla supported it, but it fell away swiftly after Constantine turned to the Christian faith in the early 4th century.

Worshippers met in underground temples (*mithraea*) and shared ritual meals, passing through seven levels of initiation in what were called the Mithraic mysteries. Key scenes found in temples and on monuments show Mithras sacrificing a bull, being born from a rock and sitting at a banquet with the Roman sun god, Sol. In Mithraic mythology, the sacrifice of the bull made possible the creation of the world. More than 400 Mithraic temples have been found, in Ostia, Rome and military outposts across the empire – in Britain and along the Rhine, for example.

# Catacombs

Early Christians in Rome buried their dead in underground cemeteries called catacombs. The name was probably first used for the underground cemetery beneath the Basilica of San Sebastian on the Appian Way in Rome, where the bodies of St Paul and the Apostle Peter (see page 318) were reputedly kept in the late 3rd century. This was then applied more generally to the many vaults below Rome in which Christians held memorial masses for the departed and celebrated the Eucharist, as part of funeral services. They also built shrines to saints, constructed chapels and hid there in times of persecution.

Historians once believed that Christians also worshipped in the catacombs, but there were too many worshippers and the crypts were too small for this to have happened frequently. Although burial of the dead was an Etruscan custom, it was not generally used by the Romans, who preferred cremation. Christians chose the practice because they believed in the bodily resurrection of believers.

# Trajan and the *Pax Romana*

Ruling 98–117 CE, Trajan (53–117 CE) was the first Roman emperor since the reign of Augustus to enlarge the Roman Empire substantially. Born in the province of Baetica (southern Spain), he rose to prominence as a military commander and was adopted by Emperor Nerva as his successor in 97 CE.

As emperor he led the army to a series of triumphs. He created a new province of Dacia in Romania and Transylvania, and tamed the troublesome Parthians, taking Armenia and northern Mesopotamia. It was said that Trajan wept when he reached the Persian Gulf because he was too old to repeat the legendary achievements of Alexander the Great in India. Despite these military campaigns, Trajan lived at the height of what historians call the *Pax Romana* ('Roman Peace') – a peaceful period from Augustus's death to the reign of Marcus Aurelius (161–180 CE). In Rome, Trajan made improvements in education and aid to poor citizens, and oversaw building works including a new aqueduct and baths, libraries, a new forum and Trajan's Column, which celebrated his victories in Dacia.

# Boundaries of Empire

At the time of Emperor Trajan's death in 117 CE, the Roman Empire was at its largest. It stretched from Britannia (England and Wales) in the north to Aegyptus (Egypt) in the south, and from Lusitania (Portugal) in the west to Armenia, Assyria and Mesopotamia (from Armenia to Iraq) in the east. This area covered 5 million km² (1.9 million square miles) and was home to between 55 and 100 million people, according to different historians. Most of this territory had been conquered during the Roman Republic (509–27 BCE). Some of Trajan's conquests in the East were very short-lived, since his successor Hadrian (reigned 117–138 CE) adopted a policy of consolidating the boundaries of empire and gave up the conquests east of the Euphrates. Hadrian's building of the famous wall across northern England to secure the northern boundary was part of this process of consolidation. The Romans believed in the 'empire without end' that, according to Virgil's *Aeneid* (see page 356), had been granted them by the god Jupiter – an empire with no necessary physical or temporal limits.

Running across the landscape of northern England, Hadrian's Wall is one of many such barriers along Roman frontiers.

# Marcus Aurelius

Roman emperor Marcus Aurelius (121–180 CE), who was in power at a troubled time for the empire and led military operations on the Danube for almost ten years, is celebrated less for his life and rule than for his *Meditations*. This was a notebook of devotional exercises and philosophy influenced by the Stoics.

As a young man being instructed in rhetoric, Aurelius was greatly influenced by the *Discourses* of the Greek philosopher Epictetus. He wrote his *Meditations* in Greek while on campaign in 170–180 CE. Their focus was on analysing one's own judgement and taking a wide perspective on events. He believed in a principle of order behind all things, and that individuals should avoid sensory overindulgence and seek to act ethically. Aurelius is generally viewed as a good ruler – in traditional accounts, the last of the 'five good emperors' who ruled 96–180 CE in the time of the *Pax Romana* (the others being Nerva, Trajan, Hadrian and Antoninus Pius).

# Rise of the Goths

The Goths, a nomadic Germanic people originally from Scandinavia and the southern Baltic, established themselves near the Black Sea in the 2nd–3rd century CE. They split into two branches, the Ostrogoths and Visigoths, and both became a thorn in the side of the Roman Empire. Each created a kingdom out of the collapse of Rome in the West. The Roman author Tacitus (see page 378) says they fought with short swords, carried round shields and were known for their loyalty to their kings. After they migrated to the Black Sea, they raided Roman provinces in Anatolia and the Balkans. The Visigoths settled in Romania, while the Ostrogoths established a large kingdom further east. Both groups were driven out by the nomadic Huns, in the late 4th century CE. The Visigoths defeated Roman emperor Valens in 378 CE at Adrianople (now Edirne, Turkey), then were settled by Emperor Theodosius I in Moesia (southern Balkans). In the early 5th century CE, they began raiding Italy and sacked Rome in 410. The Visigoths later settled in southern France and Spain while the Ostrogoths settled in Italy.

Like many peoples depicted as barbaric in Roman chronicles, the Goths in fact had a well developed culture, and were skilled metalworkers, as this jewelled belt buckle shows.

# Septimius Severus

Roman emperor Septimius Severus (145–211 CE) brought strong rule and stability after civil war and founded a dynasty that held power – with a brief interlude in 217–218 CE – for almost a quarter-century until 235 CE. Under his rule, the role of the Senate declined and the army gained power. Severus effectively established a military dictatorship. Born in Leptis Magna (now Libya), he was in command of an army on the Danube when Emperor Commodus was murdered in December 192 CE and his successor Pertinax was also killed in March 193 CE.

After his troops declared Severus emperor, he defeated rivals Pescennius Niger and Clodius Albinus, and named his son Caracalla his co-ruler and successor. In the east, he defeated a Parthian incursion and in 199 CE brought Mesopotamia back into the empire. The Arch of Septimius Severus in the Roman Forum (see page 354) commemorates this achievement. Severus died at Eboracum (York) while on an unsuccessful campaign in Britain to conquer Caledonia (Scotland).

This tondo painting from Egypt depicts Septimius Severus, his wife and sons.

# Diocletian and the division of Empire

In 286 CE, Emperor Diocletian (reigned 284–305 CE) split the Roman Empire into two parts, East and West. His aim was to restore order after a period of crisis earlier in the third century. Diocletian ruled the Eastern Empire from Nicomedia (Izmit in Turkey), and passed control of the Western Empire to the loyal Maximian, based in Milan in northern Italy. Each took the title Augustus, and Rome remained the official capital. Then, in 293 CE, under the celebrated tetrachy ('rule of four'), two junior co-rulers were added, each with the title Caesar. Constantius would assist Maximian and be based at Trier (Germany), while Galerius would serve under Diocletian and be settled in Sirmium (modern Serbia). Diocletian's reforms helped stabilize the empire, which had come close to collapse. He made the borders safe, defeated troublesome tribes and negotiated an enduring peace with Sasanian Persia, after Galerius and he sacked their capital Ctesiphon in 299 CE. He also oversaw the last major persecution of Christians in 303–311 CE and was the first Roman emperor to abdicate in 305 CE.

# Constantine the Great

Under Constantine the Great the Roman Empire became Christian. In 330 he founded a new eastern capital for the empire in Constantinople (Istanbul, Turkey). Constantine was the first emperor to declare himself a Christian and credited the Christian God with carrying him to power. He won the famous Battle of Milvian Bridge in 312 over his rival, Maxentius, after having a vision of the cross of Christ and seeing the heavenly message, 'With this sign you will win.' He is a major figure in the history of Christianity – not only issuing the Edict of Milan in 313 that decreed Christians could live free of persecution in the empire, but also calling the church council of Nicaea (now Iznik, Turkey) at which churchmen agreed the Nicene Creed as a statement of Christian doctrine. A version of the creed, which originally began: 'We believe in one God, the Father Almighty, Maker of all things visible and invisible,' is still in use today. In addition, he ordered the building of the Church of the Holy Sepulchre in Jerusalem, on the reputed site of Jesus's burial. The Eastern Orthodox Church sees him as a saint.

# The Latin Bible

Working in Rome, the scholar Eusebius Hieronymus – better known as St Jerome – made a celebrated translation of the Bible into Latin. He was secretary to Pope Damasus I, who commissioned him in 382 to make the translation. He revised existing translations of the gospels in 383, then translated the Old Testament – first using the Septuagint Greek translation as his source for parts of the work, then making a new translation from the original Hebrew. This mammoth task was not finished until 405.

Jerome was born in Stridon, Dalmatia (near Ljubljana in Slovenia), but came to Rome to study from the age of 12 and was baptized as a Christian, perhaps by Pope Liberius. He spent many years studying and lived as a hermit for a time. His Latin translation combined with other versions became known as the Vulgate (from Latin *editio vulgata*, or 'common edition') and was the most widely used version in the Western Church from the 7th century onwards. Jerome finished his life as a monk in Bethlehem.

St Jerome is often depicted with a pet lion that he supposedly tamed while living in penitential exile in the Syrian desert.

# The Sack of Rome

In August 410 CE, the Visigoths overran the city of Rome – a landmark event in the decline and fall of the Roman Empire. Under King Alaric they besieged the city, but offered to spare it in return for a yearly payment and a position of military power in the imperial hierarchy. Emperor Honorius refused and, after the city's Salarian Gate was opened by slaves, the invaders poured in and pillaged the city for three days. They plundered Rome's wealth but spared its great buildings and, Christians themselves, allowed the people to take sanctuary in churches.

By 410 CE, Rome was not the capital of the Western Empire – it had been moved to the more easily defended Ravenna, in northern Italy. But its fall was symbolic and the event sent shock waves far and wide. Christian scholar St Jerome, a former resident of Rome and secretary to Pope Damasus living in Bethlehem, was aghast. He wrote, 'Rome, once the capital of the world, is now the grave of the Roman people … the bright light of the world was put out … the Roman Empire was beheaded.'

A fanciful depiction of the Visigoth ruler Alaric surrounded by the trappings of classical civilization

# Attila the Hun

Attila, King of the Huns (reigned 434–453 CE), was one of the most formidable enemies of the Roman Empire in its last decades. He was dubbed the 'Scourge of God' by later writers. The Huns were mounted nomads who had driven out the Ostrogoths and Visigoths as they powered into southeastern Europe in the late 4th century CE. Attila, ruling with his elder brother Bleda, unleashed two devastating attacks on the Eastern Roman Empire in 441 CE and 443 CE. They sacked a string of cities, including Singidunum (Belgrade), and twice defeated a Roman army, forcing Emperor Theodosius II to agree a humiliating peace. Then, in 445 CE, Attila had Bleda murdered and ruled alone. He attacked the Eastern Empire again, in 447 CE, raiding ruthlessly as far as Thermopylae in Greece. In 451 CE, he invaded Gaul but met his match in a combined army of the Roman Empire and the Visigoths in the Battle of the Catalaunian Plains. The following year, he invaded Italy and was poised to attack Rome but was persuaded to spare the city by the personal intervention of Pope Leo I.

# Vandals

The Vandals captured Carthage and threw off Roman overlordship to set up an independent state in north Africa in 439 CE. A Germanic tribe originally from Scandinavia who settled in southern Poland, they had been driven westwards by the Huns and made their home in Gaul and then in the Iberian peninsula in the early 5th century CE. From there they migrated to North Africa, where they lived initially under Roman control. Once independent they expanded, taking Sardinia, Sicily and Corsica, while their pirate fleets ranged across the Mediterranean.

Under Gaiseric, they invaded Italy in 455 CE and famously sacked and plundered Rome for two weeks. Henceforth, their name would be a byword for wanton destruction. Their kingdom thrived until 534 CE when, after the collapse of the Roman Empire in the West, Eastern Roman emperor Justinian I recaptured their lands. The Vandals were Arian Christians, embracing the teachings of a 3rd/4th-century Egyptian priest, Arius, who stressed the supremecy of the unity of God over the notion of the Trinity.

A Vandal coin from the North African city of Carthage.

# The Roman collapse

The last Roman emperor in the west, Romulus Augustulus, was deposed in 476 CE by the Germanic warrior Odoacer, who became the first 'barbarian' King of Italy. Historians mark this collapse of the Western Roman Empire as the end of the ancient world in the West. Probably originally a member of the East Germanic Scirii tribe, Odoacer had risen to prominence in the Roman army. The ruler he deposed, Romulus Augustulus (reigned 475–476 CE), was in fact not legitimate. His father, the general Orestes, had deposed Roman emperor Julius Nepos (reigned 474–475 CE) and put Romulus on the throne. Odoacer led a revolt against Orestes and was declared king by his troops. He held power in Italy but recognized he was subject to the eastern emperor, Zeno (reigned 474–491 CE). The Western Roman Empire collapsed into rival kingdoms, but the Eastern Empire based in Constantinople would endure for almost 1,000 years. Eventually, the city – originally called Byzantium and refounded by Emperor Constantine the Great in 330 CE – was taken by the Ottoman Turks and renamed Istanbul in 1453.

Romulus Augustulus cedes power to his rebel general Odoacer — the final chapter in the story of the Western Roman Empire.

# Glossary

**Consul**
A chief magistrate in the Roman Republic. Two consuls were elected each year to serve as administrators and often also military leaders. The title was preserved after the establishment of the Roman Empire in 27 BCE, but its powers were greatly reduced.

**Cyclopes**
One-eyed giants of immense strength in ancient Greek mythology, said to be the builders of the monumental 'cyclopean' walls at Mycenaean-era Greek cities including Tiryns and Athens.

**Geoglyph**
A design made by humans in the natural landscape that is only fully visible from a distance or from above. Examples include the Uffington White Horse (c.1000 BCE), cut into the chalk downs in Oxfordshire, England, and the Paracas Candelabra carved on a sandy hillside in eastern Chile by the Paracas people (c.900 BCE–400 CE). Probably the most famous geoglyphs are the Nazca Lines, dug in the dry surface of the Pampa Colorada, southern Peru from c.200 BCE.

**Hellenization**
The spread of Greek lifestyle and culture – and in some cases of the use of Greek as a language. In the ancient world Greek culture spread throughout the empires that emerged in Macedonia, Persia and Egypt from the time of Alexander the Great to Rome's conquest of Egypt in 30 BCE.

### Hippocratic Oath

A code of behaviour for doctors and teachers of medicine, taken from papers, the Hippocratic Collection, associated with the Greek physician Hippocrates, active in the 4th and 5th centuries BCE.

### Mesoamerica

The area running from central Mexico across Guatemala and Honduras to western Nicaragua and Costa Rica. Historians apply the name to the Maya, Olmec, Zapotec, Aztec and other cultures that arose in this area between the late 3rd millennium BCE and ended with the Spanish invasion of 1521.

### Mesopotamia

The area between the Euphrates and Tigris rivers in south west Asia, now part of Iraq, where the Sumerian, Babylonian and Assyrian civilisations arose. The name comes from the Greek for 'between two rivers' but probably derives from older Aramaic and Akkadian words meaning the same thing.

### Mummification

The preservation of a dead body using processes of embalming and dessication, practised by several ancient cultures, particularly in Egypt and the Americas. In extremely arid conditions, mummification can also occur naturally.

### Papyrus

A flexible material made from the pith of the *Cyperus papyrus* sedge plant, used as a writing surface in Egypt and around the ancient Mediterranean. Papyrus was an alternative to parchment (treated animal skins that proved more durable in damp climates). Both were slowly supplanted with the spread of paper from its birthplace in China.

### Peripatetic

The name given to pupils and followers of ancient Greek philosopher Aristotle (384–322 BCE). Aristotle famously taught as he walked up and down in the Lyceum, the school he opened in Athens, and his pupils followed him as he went.

## Phalanx

A group of infantry on the battlefield, deployed standing close together and several ranks deep, with shields touching and long spears or pikes pointed forward. The Sumerian army had a phalanx six men deep and the ancient Greeks used one eight men deep. Philip II of Macedon (382–336 BCE) and his son Alexander the Great (356–323 BCE) made the unit a truly formidable weapon of war, 16 men deep.

## Plaza

A public square or marketplace, from the Spanish *plaza* ('open space'). Historians of the ancient world describe public areas in the cities of South American and Mesoamerican cultures as plazas.

## Pre-ceramic

A culture or people that has not developed the knowledge of how to fire pots. When archaeologists find no evidence of ceramics (fired pots) in the remains of a culture they designate it 'pre-ceramic'.

## Prosody

The theory of composing verses, especially rules on pronunciation and how to manage the metre (or rhythm) of verse.

## Pyramid

A form of ancient monumental building imitating an artificial hill or mountain, typically with a square base rising to a narrower top. The natural stability of the pyramid design means it arose independently in several ancient cultures, sometimes with smooth sides but more often with a stepped design. Some forms narrowed to a point (as in the famous Egyptian pyramids at Giza) while others (Mesoamerican temples and Mesopotamian ziggurats) rose to a flat platform used for ritual purposes.

## Satrapy

The Persian Achaemenid Empire was divided by Darius I 'the Great' (c.550–486 BCE) into provinces, called satrapies. They were ruled by governors called satraps, appointed by the king and responsible for collecting taxes. The word satrap comes from Old Persian, meaning 'protector of the region'. When Alexander the Great conquered the empire he kept the system, and it was also retained by his successors.

### Stele

A standing stone carved with images and inscriptions. In the ancient world they were often used to commemorate military victories, mark territory and promulgate laws or other information. Stelae are found particularly in Mesopotamia, Egypt and Mesoamerica.

### Stupas

Commemorative monuments erected by Buddhists in ancient India, with a mound-like shape probably derived from that of earlier burial mounds. Stupas were usually associated with the relics linked to the Buddha or other holy figures of Buddhism. The celebrated Great Stupa at Sanchi in central India was probably built by the Emperor Ashoka (304–232 BCE) and was decorated with carvings showing scenes from the life of and legends about the Buddha. Smaller stupas and caskets surround it.

### Theocracy

In some cultures – called theocracies by historians – ultimate authority derives from laws delivered by God or a group of gods/goddesses. In these societies, priests take a prominent role in government, interpreting and applying the divine laws.

### Vizier

In ancient Egypt, a chief minister who served the pharaoh. The office dates back to at least the 4th Dynasty (c.2575–c.2465 BCE).

### Ziggurat

A stepped pyramid-temple built in the cities of ancient Mesopotamia. The celebrated ziggurat of Ur, built in the 3rd millennium BCE, had a shrine on its top platform to the city's patron, the moon god Nanna.

# Index

First published in Great Britain in 2018 by

Quercus Editions Ltd
Carmelite House
50 Victoria Embankment
London EC4Y 0DZ

An Hachette UK company


Text by Charles Phillips

Packaged by Pikaia Imaging
Edited by Dan Green



A CIP catalogue record for this book is available from the British Library

PB ISBN 9781786485816
EBOOK ISBN 9781786485823



10 9 8 7 6 5 4 3 2 1

Printed and bound in China

2: siete_vidas via Wikimedia; 13: Shutterstock/Sezai Sahmay; 17: Editor at large via Wikimedia; 19: Schøyen Collection via Wikimedia; 21: Metropolitan Museum of Art via Wikimedia; 23: Shutterstock/Leon Rafael; 25: Shutterstock/Fotografos; 29: Re1mod via Wikimedia; 31: Osama Shukir Muhammed Amin FRCP(Glasg) via Wikimedia; 37: Musée du Louvre via Wikimedia; excavated by Ernest de Sarzec; 41: Oriental Institute at the University of Chicago via Wikimedia; 43: Shutterstock/Stig Alenas; 45: Musée du Louvre via Wikimedia; 47: Acquired by Henry Walters, 1925, via Wikimedia; 53: Jon Sullivan of PDPhoto.org via Wikimedia; 57: Ricardo Liberato via Wikimedia; 63: Neues Museum, Berlin via Wikimedia; 65: G. Elliot Smith via Wikimedia; 67: Philip Pikart via Wikimedia; 69: rob koopman via Wikimedia; 71: Gérard Ducher via Wikimedia; 73: Carsten Frenzi via Wikimedia; 75: Mujtaba Chohan via Wikimedia; 77: Shutterstock/Paolo Gallo; 79: Shutterstock/Nicku; 83: Andrew Dunn via Wikimedia; 85: Hans Hillewaert via Wikimedia; 87: Håkan Svensson Xauxa via Wikimedia; 89: Wolfgang Sauber via Wikimedia; 91: Lombards Museum via Wikimedia; 93: Maribel Ponce Ixba via Wikimedia; 95: Dtarazona via Wikimedia; 97: USDA Agricultural Stabilization and Conservation Service via Wikimedia; 99: Brooklyn Museum via Wikimedia; 101: Matt Murphy via Wikimedia; 103: Tim Kiser via Wikimedia; 107: Diego Delso, delso.photo via Wikimedia; 111: Legs Louis Capitan via Wikimedia; 113: Shutterstock/Galaro; 115: Shutterstock/Zack Frank; 117: Shutterstock/Andrea Delbo; 119: Shutterstock/Paulo Afonso; 121: Shutterstock/akolye; 123: Shutterstock/Vadim Petrakov; 125: Ansgar Walk via Wikimedia; 127: icelight via Wikimedia; 131: Robur.q via Wikimedia; 133: Jebulon via Wikimedia; 135: Xuan Che via Wikimedia; 137: Yann Forget via Wikimedia; 139: Travelling Runes via Wikimedia; 141: Jastrow via Wikimedia; 147: Shutterstock/Anastasios71; 149: Jastrow via Wikimedia; 153: Masur via Wikimedia; 157: Paolo Monti via Wikimedia; 161: Shutterstock/sianstock; 165: Shutterstock/Anastasios71; 167: Shutterstock/Onischenko Natalya; 169: Shutterstock/Free Wind 2014; 175: Shutterstock/Serghei Starus; 177: Wellcome Images via Wikimedia; 179: Shutterstock/muratart; 181: Sarah Murray via Wikimedia; 185: Eric Gaba via Wikimedia; 199: Ess ech via Wikimedia; 201: Gunawan Kartapranata via Wikimedia; 205: CNG Coins via Wikimedia; 207: Christophe Meneboeuf via Wikimedia; 209: Rajeshphy1727 via Wikimedia; 213: Christopher J. Fynn via Wikimedia; 215: CNG Coins via Wikimedia; 219: sailko via Wikimedia; 221: Heaven's Army via Wikimedia; 225: Ernst Stavro Blofeld via Wikimedia; 227: Pratyeka via Wikimedia; 235: Larsbo c via Wikimedia; 237: Mountain via Wikimedia; 243: Maros Mraz via Wikimedia; 245: Herbert Ponting via Wikimedia; 247: Editor at Large via Wikimedia; 251: TKostolany via Wikimedia; 261: Shutterstock/cowardlion; 265: Shutterstock/Kanuman; 267: Jebulon via Wikimedia; 269: Walters Art Museum via Wikimedia; 271: Osama Shukir Muhammed Amin FRCP(Glasg) via Wikimedia; 281: Acquired by Henry Walters, 1929, via Wikimedia; 283: Jastrow via Wikimedia; 287: Urek Meniashvili via Wikimedia; 289: Carole Raddato via Wikimedia; 291: reibai via Wikimedia; 297: CNG Coins via Wikimedia; 301: dynamosquito via Wikimedia; 303: Roodiparse via Wikimedia; 305: Shutterstock/Morphart Creation; 307: CNG Coins via Wikimedia; 313: Shutterstock/eFesenko; 315: Andrew Shiva / Wikipedia / CC BY-SA 4.0; 317: Israel Museum via Wikimedia; 319: Rogers Fund, 1943 via Wikimedia; 321: Marie-Lan Nguyen via Wikimedia; 325: The Education Center of the National Library of Israel via Wikimedia; 329: Marie-Lan Nguyen via Wikimedia; 331: Wellcome Images via Wikimedia; 333: Marie-Lan Nguyen via Wikimedia; 337: Miguel Hermoso Cuesta via Wikimedia; 339: CNG Coins via Wikimedia; 345: GuidoB via Wikimedia; 347: Gautier Poupeau via Wikimedia; 349: Bibi Saint-Pol via Wikimedia; 353: Cassius Ahenobarbus via Wikimedia; 355: sailko via Wikimedia; 361: sailko via Wikimedia; 363: Louis le Grand via Wikimedia; 365: Clio20 via Wikimedia; 369: © Marie-Lan Nguyen / Wikimedia Commons / CC-BY 2.5; 371: Shutterstock/Claudio Divizia; 373: Livioandronico2013 via Wikimedia; 375: Morn the Gorn via Wikimedia; 377: Walters Art Museum via Wikimedia; 381: Serge Ottaviani via Wikimedia; 383: Shutterstock/David Soanes; 385: Wolfgang Sauber via Wikimedia; 387: Shutterstock/Panglossian; 389: Pierre-Selim via Wikimedia; 391: Acquired by Henry Walters, via Wikimedia; 395: G.dallorto via Wikimedia; 405: DrFO.Jr.Tn via Wikimedia.